"Continuing the work of James McGregor Burns' seminal work on history and leadership is certainly overdue and a worthwhile undertaking. Blincoe and Shoup's use of historical context underscores the critical nature of organizational leadership and culture. This work appeals to both the practitioner and student of leadership."

– **Paul M. McInerny,** *Marquette University, USA*

"In times of crisis, crucial decisions taken by leaders shape the course of history. What do leaders draw on? Here Blincoe and Shoup cogently argue the case that lessons from history provide a valuable context that both informs and underpins decision-making. Building on the pioneering study of leadership by James McGregor Burns, this concise work deftly connects the study (and understanding) of history with the principles and dynamics of leadership and management."

– **Norman Abjorensen,** *The Australian National University, Australia*

History and Leadership

Leaders and managers are rightly tasked to take their organizations and communities to a desired future. They are expected to be forward looking with compelling vision statements. As a result, they are often too busy in the present managing the future to be bothered with the past. Yet it is organizational histories that provide the contexts and clues for the future. *History and Leadership: The Nature and Role of the Past in Navigating the Future* demonstrates that intentional historical perspective-taking provides a sort of wisdom for doing business in the present and future and equips leaders to leverage the past to help their organizations thrive.

This book appeals to several audiences. It will serve as a supplementary text for undergraduate and graduate students in both the humanities and leadership studies. The book also appeals to practicing leaders and managers who wish to develop their emotional, cultural, and social intelligence by exploring perennial issues and lessons found in well-developed histories. This book also serves as a stand-alone read for a range of professionals who want a more recreational and non-traditional read on history and leadership. The book cultivates an appreciation for history and equips readers to be connoisseurs of history for the betterment of themselves and society.

Mark E. Blincoe, PhD, is Professor of History at California Baptist University and Leadership Fellow with the Dr. Paul & Annie Kienel Leadership Institute.

John R. Shoup, PhD, is Professor of Leadership Studies at California Baptist University and the Executive Director of the Dr. Paul & Annie Kienel Leadership Institute.

Leadership Horizons
Series Editors
John Shoup and Troy Hinrichs
California Baptist University, USA

The original and timeless research on leadership is situated in the classical works associated with the humanities. Great literature, art, theatre, philosophy, and music provide both existential and visceral insights to the drama of leadership beyond what traditional approaches to leadership studies have been able to furnish up to now. The classics in the humanities are didactic commentaries on universal themes associated with the challenges and hopes of good leadership. Knowledge of the classics provides a way of appreciating historical and contemporary cultures and a framework for thinking deeply about what is true, good, honorable, and beautiful. Returning the classics to the leadership genre equips leaders with a culturally informed language and narrative to develop the often ignored aesthetical aspects of leadership. This series connects lessons from various great works in art, literature, philosophy, theatre, and music to specific leadership research and contemporary leadership challenges. The series weaves the art and science of leadership studies and equip readers with multiple frames of reference to become aesthetically pleasing, engaging, and culturally astute leaders to make the right things happen the right way.

Leadership Horizons is relevant to students and researchers across business and management, organizational and institutional studies, and the humanities.

Books in the series:

Literature and Leadership
The Role of Narrative in Organizational Sensemaking
John R. Shoup and Troy W. Hinrichs

Philosophy and Leadership
Three Classical Models and Cases
Brent Edwin Cusher and Mark Antonio Menaldo

History and Leadership
The Nature and Role of the Past in Navigating the Future
Mark E. Blincoe and John R. Shoup

History and Leadership

The Nature and Role of the Past in Navigating the Future

Mark E. Blincoe and John R. Shoup

Routledge
Taylor & Francis Group

NEW YORK AND LONDON

First published 2023
by Routledge
605 Third Avenue, New York, NY 10158

and by Routledge
4 Park Square, Milton Park, Abingdon, Oxon, OX14 4RN

Routledge is an imprint of the Taylor & Francis Group, an informa business

Library of Congress Cataloging-in-Publication Data
Names: Blincoe, Mark E., author. | Shoup, John R., author.
Title: History and leadership : the nature and role of the past in navigating
    the future / Mark E. Blincoe and John R. Shoup.
Description: New York, NY : Routledge, 2023. | Includes bibliographical
    references and index.
Identifiers: LCCN 2022011317 | ISBN 9780367569785 (hardback) |
    ISBN 9780367569822 (paperback) | ISBN 9781003100171 (ebook)
Subjects: LCSH: Leadership. | Management.
Classification: LCC HD57.7 .B568 2022 | DDC 658.4/092—
    dc23/eng/20220314
LC record available at https://lccn.loc.gov/2022011317

ISBN: 978-0-367-56978-5 (hbk)
ISBN: 978-0-367-56982-2 (pbk)
ISBN: 978-1-003-10017-1 (ebk)

DOI: 10.4324/9781003100171

Typeset in Times New Roman
by Apex CoVantage, LLC

To Kristen Blincoe, for your constant love and support; and to Robert, for your patience and interest. – Mark

To Rebecca Joy Shoup, the real historian in the family. – Dad

Contents

Author Biographies

Mark E. Blincoe is Professor of History as well as a Fellow at the Dr. Paul and Annie Kienel Leadership Institute at California Baptist University in Riverside, California. Mark teaches European history, historiography, and historical research at the undergraduate level. His academic field pertains to medieval history, though his training and interests extend into the modern era. Mark earned his PhD degree in history at the University of Minnesota. He also holds an MA degree in history from the University of Pennsylvania and BA in history and sociology from Whitworth University in Spokane, WA. He has been married for over 25 years to Kristen and has one son, Robert.

John R. Shoup is the Executive Director of the Dr. Paul and Annie Kienel Leadership Institute at California Baptist University in Riverside. He also teaches leadership and educational history and policy at the graduate level and has conducted research and workshops on leadership development and best practices. John has served as a university dean, middle and high school principal, and social worker in various service settings. He is an author and frequent presenter on topics related to leadership. John has a PhD degree in Education with an emphasis in Educational Administration and Policy Studies from the University of California, Riverside. He also has a Master of Divinity and a Master of Arts in Counseling Psychology from Trinity Evangelical Divinity School in Deerfield, IL. He has been married for 33 years to Margarita and has one daughter, Rebecca.

Preface

On March 1, 2021, John Pepper, former CEO of Proctor & Gamble and former Chairman of the Board at the Walt Disney Company, published an Op-Ed with his local newspaper, *Springfield News-Sun*, in response to changes in the Liberal Arts program at Wright State University in Ohio. In the midst of his discussion on the value of the history major, he offers some sage advice from his decades of experience as a corporate leader. He wrote, "if great institutions are to survive and grow, they must achieve a balance between preserving the core values that enabled past success, while being able to evolve and adapt to changing circumstances." In his opinion, the study of history is the best way to meet the challenges of a complex world.

That history is important is evidenced by the fact that it is a required subject in schools and colleges. However, when people enter their professional lives, history competes with the demands of the present. Even if one was to find discretionary time to do history, the computer, television, movies, and other activities are often more enticing forms of relaxation than reading a history book or visiting a museum. Yet people are by nature amateur historians and would be lost without their own historical awareness. Why is it people love to reminisce? Why do people keep family albums and heirlooms? People have and need a sense of "self" in relationship to others in place and time, not only to fit in but to thrive according to established rules, customs, and norms. The past is a major source, often the core, of individual and collective identities. Shared history is what provides people and organizations a sense of continuity with the past, identity in the present, and direction for the future.

History is a unique mentor. It provides a type of hindsight that gives insight for today and foresight for tomorrow. This book establishes that the pursuit of history offers wisdom for doing business and equips leaders to leverage the past to help their organizations thrive. Leaders and managers are tasked with creating solutions to new challenges while anticipating future problems. They are expected to be forward thinking. Yet all decisions come from previous experiences, lessons learned from the past, and earlier organizational models that can be adapted to new circumstances. History provides the contexts and clues to discern the proper trajectories for the future.

An important premise of this book is that leaders and managers who think and act like historians will have deeper wells of knowledge and understanding from which to make meaningful comparisons, and subsequently better judgment calls, about people and events. History is instructive in that it reveals patterns in human behavior that transcend time. It also points to shared values that provide organizations a sense of continuity through changing circumstances. Historians are trained to build an understanding of people within their own context, determine the factors that shaped their decisions, and evaluate the impact of those decisions on the immediate and distant future. They also identify parallel experiences across time to compare how people managed similar dilemmas. As a way of knowing, history does far more than explain why things happen. It offers a vast experience beyond what any individual can generate through their own personal encounters.

There are several compelling reasons why history is important (and entertaining) at the individual and organizational levels. Rick Paulas (2018, January 2) notes that corporate history is a way for companies to reinforce their culture and differentiate themselves from other institutions. Organizational history provides relevant stories that promote a sense a belonging. It can be used as the center of corporate identity, creating a sense of loyalty and pride among an organization's stakeholders. The anonymous Bartleby with *The Economist* (2018, August 25) notes that a broader sense of history provides valuable insight into leadership. The author notes that studying political leaders like Otto Von Bismark, Franklin Delano Roosevelt, and Winston Churchill provide case studies on effective leadership in context that can be applied to a corporate environment. Holger Seim (2015, May 19), the CEO of the Berlin-based learning company Blinkist, suggests that young CEOs study a variety of past leaders to build the confidence to develop their organizations.

History trains the mind to identify patterns, understand trends, and make meaningful comparisons that are useful when planning for the future. This book will establish the connection between history and good leadership, encouraging leaders to cultivate a historical mindset. This focus on history is especially appropriate since the creation of an academic discipline devoted to the study and practice of leadership was launched by the renowned historian James McGregor Burns. The book is written as a resource to help leaders understand why and how to think like historians. It is also written to historians as an example to make history more relevant.

This book is part of the *Routledge Leadership Horizons* series that reintroduces art, literature, theatre, music, and philosophy into the leadership and management studies genres. Good history can serve as didactic commentaries on the patterns and themes that shape life and provide poignant lessons on leadership. Understanding how history is crafted positions readers to be sophisticated historians who can construct and leverage their groups' usable past to create an esprit de corps that in turn solidifies group identities and optimizes engagement and performance. The book strives to make history more accessible and relevant for emerging and established leaders. It also illustrates how leaders and managers can be sophisticated historians, leveraging the past as an invisible mentor for themselves and their organizations.

The following discussion establishes a bridge between the study of history and ongoing research in leadership and management. Chapter one explains the discipline of history and how it matters. It demonstrates how history makes the past knowable and usable, highlighting three of its most crucial functions: sensemaking, a source of guidance, and identity formation. This chapter encourages readers to cultivate a historical mindset and introduces how this applies for business leaders. Chapter two offers some historical grounding on the principles developed in the first chapter. It provides a brief overview on important aspects of the Renaissance, Enlightenment, and Industrial Revolution to illustrate by example how history makes sense of the past by contextualizing trends, assesses the impact of human ideas and actions, and explains their short- and long-term significance. The examples used to represent these historical movements capture the essence of their eras and align with the book's overall focus on organizational leadership.

Chapter three explains why organizations exist and how they function as they do and give leaders and managers a sense of their own professional contexts. The chapter explores the evolution of organizations, offering a history of the formal and informal rules and practices that both liberate and constrain organizational leaders and managers. It argues that the logics of governing organizational life are rooted in history, which offers implications and best practices for leaders and managers to optimize their collective workforce. Chapter four applies history to field of leadership studies and the practice of organizational leadership. In particular, the chapter highlights history's role in facilitating emotional and social intelligence, allowing leaders to make connections with their stakeholders and promote organizational identity, foster loyalty, and reinforce core values. It also illustrates how history can serve a diagnostic role for future planning, establishing patterns that identify a sense of continuity that are essential to organizational strength, but also isolating cycles that can help leaders anticipate future trends.

The final chapter provides case studies from successful companies that deliberately leverage the past to reinforce corporate identity and shape organizational strategies. The Watkins Company (f. 1868), Edwards Life-sciences (f. 1958), and The Walt Disney Company (f. 1923) illustrate that leaders who understand their company's history are able to effectively maintain the core mission of their organizations while managing change. These companies were selected because they are diverse in size and purpose, highlighting that the principles expressed in this book resonate universally. Each section provides an overview of the company's history, followed by a select discussion on the way current leadership used the past to create stability and move forward in new directions. The authors of this book were able to secure interviews with the CEOs of The Watkins Company and Edwards Lifesciences. Information on Bob Iger's leadership of Disney was obtained through his own writing and public interviews.

This book is aimed at several audiences. It appeals to practicing leaders and managers who wish to develop their emotional, cultural, and social intelligence by exploring perennial issues and lessons found in well-developed histories. For those in leadership and management studies, the book reintroduces the value and methods of historical sensemaking to better understand people and events, structure goals, guide aspirations, manage complexity and ambiguity beyond what is found in the more traditional leadership and management books. Those in the humanities should find that the book makes the study of history more relevant by pointing to ways that the past can be applied to contemporary pursuits. Ultimately, this book services a wide array of professionals and students who want a greater appreciation for history or who desire a more recreational and non-traditional read on history and leadership. The book cultivates an appreciation for history and equips readers to look at the past in new ways for the betterment of themselves and society.

References

Bartleby (2018, August 25). History lessons for managers. *The Economist*. www.economist.com/business/2018/08/23/history-lessons-for-managers

Paulas, Rick. (2018, January 2). How corporations use history to their advantage. *Pacific Standard Magazine*. https://psmag.com/economics/how-corporations-use-history-to-their-advantage

Pepper, John. (2021, March 1). Opinion: America and the world needs history majors. *Springfield News-Sun*. www.springfieldnewssun.com/local/opinion-america-and-the-world-need-history-majors/4C6LC4JMLZAE7GJG4MKXDCJY3A/

Seim, Holger. (2015, May 19). Lessons for the new CEO from 5 great leaders of history. *Entrepreneur*. www.entrepreneur.com/article/246388

Acknowledgments

Thank you to Mark Jacobs, CEO of The Watkins Co., and Mike Mussallem, CEO of Edwards Life Sciences, for sharing their histories and wisdom.

Thank you to Abigail Bello for her editorial work and keeping the authors on task.

1 The Nature and Role of History in the Humanities and Leadership Studies

Introduction

The past is a consummate teacher if properly understood. It offers innumerable case studies on the way people interact, respond to their environment, and organize their lives. Because of this, historians since ancient times have frequently dedicated books to their leaders, hoping that the past would become a source of wisdom for good leadership. This chapter builds on the notion that historical knowledge can develop better leaders. Evaluating leadership in both the past and the present requires understanding the broader historical context that shapes decisions and transforms organizations. The larger aim here is to demonstrate that the pursuit of history itself is an important aspect of good leadership. Leaders and managers who think historically will make more meaningful comparisons, and subsequently better judgment calls, when developing strategies for the future.

While every organization has a past, a series of activities and relationships that took place at an earlier time, it is the history built from this past that defines organizations and sets them apart. History forms an organization's identity, shapes its values, establishes its reputation, and offers experience that helps leaders make wise decisions. An organization's history is also deeply embedded in the larger social, political, and economic settings that influence its scope and function. Those with a clearer understanding of the way that the present is connected to the past will make better decisions.

This chapter introduces the general characteristics of good history and how it matters for leaders and managers. The basic premise is that the practice of history, as done by historians, can and should be applied by those outside of the historical profession. History is a process of investigation that seeks to understand the past in a way that is meaningful to the present. To be meaningful means that history needs to be relevant; to be relevant means that it can be used to address immediate concerns. History explains events within their own context while also searching for patterns that transcend

DOI: 10.4324/9781003100171-1

time. The past often leaves an imprint on the future or offers parallel scenarios to contemporary settings. When done well, history makes connections between people and organizations across time and space. It establishes a link between the past and the present that situates contemporary problems as part of a longer continuum. If applied appropriately, it allows leaders to better understand and relate to their colleagues and stakeholders, discern possible outcomes from their decisions, and capitalize on the momentum of the past to create desired futures.

History as a Means of Generating Good Leadership

There is nothing new about pointing to the value of history for developing good leadership. History has often been aimed at an elite audience, generally written by those who have the time and leisure to investigate the past and the status to convey their ideas to those in leadership. Ancient and medieval historians pointed to the past as a source of wisdom to guide future decisions. They presented leaders in action, offering scenarios that tested the characteristics of good and bad leadership. The medieval historian Henry of Huntingdon (2002) wrote to his peers that history should "not only provoke men of the spirit to what is good and deter them from evil, but even encourage worldly men to good deeds and reduce their wickedness." He argued that history "brings the past into view as though it were present, and allows judgement of the future by representing the past" (p. 4).

Renaissance historians expanded upon this by using history as a test against the moral failures of their own leaders. They believed the ancient past contained models that should be emulated. Their contemporary histories judged how well recent leaders embraced or deviated from the time-honored virtues of effective leadership as exemplified by Roman statesmen and Christian values. Historians like Leonardo Bruni completed studies about the ancient past and the development of Renaissance Florence in the 14th and early 15th centuries. He and his peers wrote history "as a guide for literate statesmen in search of surefire recipes for success" (Ianziti, 2012, p. 6). This presumed that leaders and their supporters should have a deep knowledge of ancient history to form a standard basis for historical judgment. History became one of the essential features of a humanist education in the 15th and 16th centuries to ensure that it could be employed by a growing number of educated professionals.

The overall goals and breadth of history have shifted since the Renaissance. Greater accessibility to education has broadened the areas of interest among historians and their audience. Yet all history is valuable for those in leadership. The issues historians write about ultimately intersect with the demands of political life, religious life, and business life. For example, any leader dealing with issues of race and gender as part of organizational strategy needs to engage with at least the results of historical inquiry, if not some of these studies themselves. Making productive changes to existing policies requires some knowledge of previous dynamics within societal networks. This requires an understanding of the research done by others and an investigation into the trends represented within an organization. Thus, history serves as a type of advisor to those in leadership. It presents different scenarios as a test for current dilemmas and offers a type of hindsight that shows possible outcomes to different solutions.

In recent years history has been valuable in demonstrating the nature of effective leadership. John McGregor Burn's seminal book on *Leadership* (1978) is the foundation for this approach. The book highlights the experiences of Woodrow Wilson, Mahatma Gandhi, Nikolai Lenin, and Adolf Hitler, though its main aim is to elucidate the historical factors that enabled a variety of leaders to gain a political following and achieve their goals. To accomplish this Burns evaluates social and intellectual history from the period of the Enlightenment (18th century) onwards and establishes their influence on political developments. He sees effective leadership in any political model as an outgrowth of historical causation and shared values. Leaders must operate within the boundaries of previous events and the decisions made by earlier leaders. They must represent the values and goals of their followers, which are also shaped by a long trajectory of historical developments.

Burns was an advocate for transformational leadership in politics, though his ideas can certainly apply to non-political organizations as well. His book works because it grounds his theories in real experiences, not simply the methods of prominent leaders, but the values and expectations of those who supported those leaders. Furthermore, he presents historical case studies that were familiar to his original audience of the late 1970s: the American and French Revolutions, democratic reform movements of the 19th and 20th centuries, U.S. Presidential leadership, Nazi Germany, Communist Russia, etc. These developments led directly to the issues of his time, and they continue to influence global politics in the 21st century. More importantly, he binds good leadership to the past. Decisions that bring useful change have roots in the developments that shape social and cultural expectations. Burns uses history to build an understanding of the hopes and goals of those who sought leadership. He frames successful leadership around the promises made by their leaders to fulfill those needs.

These ideas generated a new academic discipline in leadership studies. A popular application of this approach is to illustrate the principles of good leadership through the study of individual leaders in historical context. These are accessible because they tell a personal story and offer a good point of entry into a historical period. They also humanize the past and make it easier to connect with events that seem remote. This concept has ancient roots. The Roman historian Suetonius wrote short biographies of Julius Caesar and the first 11 emperors, using the same metrics to evaluate each person's leadership: education, hobbies, skills, ethics, friendships, reputation, achievements, and the circumstances of their rule. This model became very influential in the Middle Ages and was copied by Charlemagne's biographer Einhard, who wanted to situate the German emperor in the context of Roman standards of leadership. Neither historian simply wanted to tell stories about previous leaders. The goal was to illustrate important attributes of leadership that could be applied by current leaders to their own unique circumstances.

Contemporary historians present more sophisticated studies on leadership than their ancient and medieval peers. Yet their objectives remain the same. Doris Kearns Goodwin (2018) frames a recent study, *Leadership: in Turbulent Times*, around the experiences of four Presidents of the United States: Abraham Lincoln, Theodore Roosevelt, Franklin Delano Roosevelt, and Lyndon Johnson. Her main goal is to demonstrate how they became more effective leaders through adversity, though the questions she asks seek insight into attributes that can be applied universally. Nancy Koehn (2017) takes a similar approach in *Forged in Crisis*, extending her examples beyond the political realm by placing Abraham Lincoln alongside leaders in other areas of influence: British explorer Ernest Shackleton, who led his crew home after being marooned in a shipwreck in 1915; African American abolitionist Frederick Douglass, who became a champion for equal rights in 19th century America; German pastor Dietrich Bonhoeffer, who helped lead a resistance movement against the Nazis in World War II; and biologist and environmental activist Rachal Carson, whose book *Silent Spring* launched a new age in environmental activism in the 1960s. Koehn's goal is to illustrate that the principles of good leadership in times of crisis are the same regardless of profession or organization.

Historians have always produced history with the hope that their leaders would put it to use. It continues to serve a didactic function, offering a repository of information that can be recalled when facing new scenarios. Recent efforts have integrated history with theoretical approaches on effective leadership. These represent the historian's quest to shape contemporary leadership. It requires that their leaders understand the value of history and are prepared to use it to guide their organizations.

Characteristics of History

History is both a professional craft and the assembled knowledge of the past. It is a process of investigation that reconstructs information left behind in writings and cultural artifacts to better understand human motives and behavior. This involves the collection of data from diverse resources, analyzing this information within the context of its historical setting, and evaluating how these reflect the short- and long-term significance of human actions and ideas. This results in the development of historical narratives that explain human developments over time.

These narratives also serve as a catalyst for further research. Historians establish case studies to test prevailing assumptions about the past, building off each other's work to validate or challenge existing methods and theories. Narratives are constructed around the main arguments contained in case studies. The substance of history serves as a means of illustration, providing real experiences to highlight the impact and significance of previous events. History is not about describing events themselves. It explains how events came about, their influence, and the new contexts generated from their consequences. Historical debates about which events are more significant than others reflect ongoing arguments over which parts of the past are most relevant.

The novelist Elizabeth Mackintosh, who published under the pseudonym Josephine Tey, likened historical investigation to detective work. One of her last novels featured her main protagonist, Detective Alan Grant, as a medical patient stuck in the hospital nursing a broken leg. *The Daughter of Time* (1951) features Detective Grant passing time by investigating whether Richard III killed his nephews to inherit the English throne in 1483. Grant tests the historical narratives written by supporters of King Henry VIII during the early 16th century that claim Richard was responsible for the disappearance of Edward IV's heirs. He determines that there was no contemporary evidence pointing to Richard III as the murderer. These accusations first appeared later, in hindsight, by those loyal to the Tudor cause. Reports that the boys were missing only took place after Henry VII had defeated his cousin in battle, which led Grant to declare Richard III was innocent of the crime.

This story conveys a real historical debate about the relationship between Richard III, his family, and the political challenges of the Wars of the Roses in 15th-century England. To this day historians have yet to reach an agreement about Richard III's association with his nephews' disappearance. It highlights the way historians test assumptions about the past through the validation and cross-examination of primary resources.[1] The professionalization of history in the 19th century relied on document analysis to test the veracity of narrative accounts and taught that resources should be evaluated as reflections of their own age. The German historian Leopold Van Ranke and his peers were concerned with accuracy and objectivity. They viewed history as a type of science that followed specific rules for the investigation, analysis, and production of historical writing. Van Ranke defined history as an inductive process, the pursuit of particulars in the past from which to build an understanding of the conditions by which people lived. The goal was to learn the past on its own terms, to show history "as it was." History was about explaining the forces that brought people together and shaped human action.

Most historians today see the type of methodologies represented in 19th-century historiography[2] as a starting point for further historical investigation. Few pursue history simply to gain a stronger knowledge about the past. As Edward Carr (1961) notes, "to praise a historian for his accuracy is like praising an architect for using well-seasoned timber or properly mixed concrete in his building. It is a necessary condition of his work, but not his essential function" (p. 8). History is a process of discovery and explanation. Historians search for new sources of information and pose alternative questions to existing resources to make sense of why things happen and to create a better understanding of the human condition. The primary goal is to explain why the past matters. Historians view their work as applicable to those in other professions, regardless of whether they are in positions of leadership. The following table represents some of the main ways historians define the nature of history and its role. These categories are not intended to be mutually exclusive.

What is history?	What is history for?
Collected knowledge about the past	Source of wisdom and inspiration
Reconstruction of the past	Sense of identity and belonging
Investigation into the past	Lessons to guide future actions
Search for understanding from the past	Form of sensemaking

Historians generally recognize that the study of history should be beneficial. They hold to some common assumptions that make the past more relatable and useful. The pursuit of history assumes that people in the past are not fundamentally different than people in the present. This enables historians to search for commonalities across time that can be applied toward the future. It allows the past to be a source of wisdom and establishes a connection between people who live hundreds if not thousands of years apart. The past can only provide object lessons if human desires and motivations are similar across time. Yet historians are also aware that similarities do not mean sameness. It is easy to identify differences between people who lived in separate time-frames even when they come from the same region of the world. History relies on contextualization to unpack the complex networks of ideas, attitudes, and circumstances that shape human interaction. This allows history to become a form of sensemaking to explain the factors that shape human events.

This does not mean that historians always agree about methodology or the proper use of history.[3] Debates over the nature of history reflect the profession's development as an art and a science. Some historians view history as an objective pursuit of knowledge that parallels the social sciences. This perspective views history as a mechanism to trace patterns of behavior across time, which can give insight into contemporary observations about people and their communities. History uses the past as a type of human laboratory. It represents real-life behavior at a societal level that is impossible to replicate in a controlled experiment. Since the behavioral sciences seek universal explanations, their theories can only be accurate if they transcend time. Historians recognize that people across time lived in different situations, but they had similar concerns and responded to their own controversies and crises in ways that are like people living today. According to this view, history is about discovering universal experiences within a series of unique phenomena. When that happens, a historian can test human experiences across many settings to find patterns that can apply to the future.

A good example of this approach is Emily Erikson's *Between Monopoly and Free Trade* (2014), a study of the English East India Company's organizational structure during the 17th and 18th centuries. It focuses on the company's use of private trade allowances for employees, which enabled individuals to go around the trade monopoly that was granted by the English monarchy. Erikson adapts analytical sociology to her historical analysis to use the East India Company as a case study to understand the role of networks in organizational development. The study investigates:

> how organizational decentralization and the intertwining of private and Company interests aboard the voyages of the East Indiamen ships both encouraged exploration of new market opportunities and created a powerful internal network of communication that effectively integrated Company operations across the East.
>
> (p. 2)

The book intersects with organizational theory and economics, particularly network analysis and new institutionalism, the latter emphasizing the importance of social institutions as a key aspect of economic growth. By tying her research to contemporary discussions about organizational effectiveness, Erikson not only shows that decentralization through private trade enabled the East India Company to succeed, but she also points to the company as a relevant model for organizational development today. It is a historical study intended to provide real-world answers to problems relating to global trade and engages the theories introduced later in chapter three.

On the other end of the spectrum, many historians treat the discipline less as a science and more as an art, reflecting the personal interests and interpretations of individual historians and their audience. It is for this reason that some historians view history as a more subjective pursuit aimed at applying the past toward present concerns. History is seen as a form of literary discourse that recreates and repurposes the information gained from historical sources. John Lukacs (2012) describes the task of a historian this way:

> The historian, like the novelist, tells a story; a story of some portion of the past; he describes (rather than defines). The novelist has it easier: he can invent people who did not exist and events that did not happen. The historian cannot describe people and events that did not exist; he must limit himself to men and women who really lived; he must depend on evidences of their acts and words – though, like the novelist, he too must surmise something about their minds. In one word: to *essay*: a word that is close to "assay" but is more than that: not only weighing the evidence but attempting to find its meaning.
>
> (pp. 109–110)

Historians are tasked with communicating the essence of historical information to make it understandable and convey its meaning. History is not relativistic in that the past is different for different people, but its significance can vary based on time and perspective. This transforms the writing of history into a rhetorical exercise and often leads to debates about human motivation and the factors that shape human life.

William Dalrymple's *The Anarchy* (2019), a study of the East India Company's subjugation of India during the 18th century, reflects this type of historical writing. It is a character-driven narration on the collapse of the Mughal Empire of India and the way the East India Company profited from its demise. The book tells a story, as Dalrymple puts it,

> of how the Company defeated its principal rivals . . . to take under its own wing the Emperor Shah Alam, a man whose fate it was to witness the entire story of the Company's fifty-year-long assault on India and its rise from a humble trading company to a fully fledged imperial power.
>
> (p. xxxi)

Dalrymple emphasizes the Indian perspective on this transition, particularly Shah Alam's, as a means of illustrating the impact of company policies on subjugated territories. At the same time, the book is also rooted in the author's reflection on corporate bailouts during the financial crisis of 2007–2009. Dalrymple uses the East India Company's management of its

Indian assets as an example of corporate greed. General comparisons to today's corporate settings are made sparingly, mainly in the introduction and epilogue to the book. These serve to frame the larger significance of the study, a lesson in the author's eyes about the dangers of unregulated business on the global stage.

Despite the various leanings of individual historians, history generally reflects aspects of both the arts and sciences. It is at once an investigation aimed at explaining human behavior while also a type of retelling of the past, albeit non-fiction, with the goal of teaching how people should interact with each other and the world. Erikson and Dalrymple produced different types of studies that reflect the dual nature of history. They shared the goal of investigating the East India Company in a way that resonates with contemporary issues. In this regard, each historian presents the organization as a case study that should factor into future decision making. Neither historian can make their research directly applicable to the reader. This requires that the reader translate the various lessons derived from these studies into their own settings. Erikson demonstrates that a decentralized approach to organizing trade benefited the East India Company, intersecting current arguments relating to organizational theory, which the leadership of any specific company can apply to their own setting. Likewise, the implications of Dalrymple's research into the practices of the East India Company can lead to a variety of solutions to forestall corporate abuse.

This reflects an essential feature in the practice of history: the relationship between past, present, and future. Any effort at planning for the future requires understanding the patterns that shape the present. As the historian John Lewis Gaddis (2008) remarks: "We know the future only by the past we project into it. . . . History, in a sense, is all we have" (p. 3). History cannot predict the future, but it can use the past to explain current trends and point to potential trajectories or outcomes based on previous experiences. It can also use parallel experiences from the past to evaluate current ideas and actions, identifying consistent values and practices that bind organizations and build success through the generations. History can take various roles in building a picture that is both faithful to the past and useful for present purposes.

History as a Form of Sensemaking

Explaining human actions through the circumstances people face is one of the more important functions of historical investigation. Most people fall back to this idea of history when they encounter a crisis. This was the case in 2004 when people flocked to bookstores to buy *The 9/11 Commission Report* to read the results of the official U.S. investigation into the causes of the terrorist attacks that hit the United States on September 11, 2001. What they found was an inquiry into the development of Al Qaeda in the 1980s and 1990s, the terrorist organization's record of global violence, and the inadequacies of U.S. counterterrorism efforts to contain the expansion of Islamic terrorism and mitigate its spread to the Americas. The report relied heavily on the pursuit of history, an inquiry into an exhaustive array of government sources through which the members of the commission sought to explain why 9/11 happened. Moreover, the commission used this history to propose ways for the U.S. government to change its approach to terrorism, viewing the past with "Foresight – and Hindsight."

Searching for the reasons an event took place, or to explain disruptions to normalcy, is seldom simple. It requires:

- understanding the background or context to a particular event and the people involved
- an analysis of the tensions that serve as a catalyst to change
- a discussion about the events most important to understand how these tensions were resolved
- an explanation on how the outcome of these events moved people in a new direction

Consider, for example, Adolph Hitler's effort to recreate a unified German state and its role in shaping World War II. He built the Nazi party specifically for this goal and saw fascism as the most effective means to achieve German solidarity (along with the expulsion or elimination of all other ethnic groups, particularly the Jews). It is easy to point to a series of climatic events that led to his ability to take power and prosecute a European-wide war: German defeat in World War I (1918–1919), the Munich Putsch against the Bavarian government (1923), Hitler's authorship of *Mien Kampf* (1924), the beginning of the Great Depression (1929–30), the Nazi's party's electoral victory (1932), the burning of the Reichstag (1933), the Munich Agreement (1938), Kristallnacht (1938), and the invasions of Czechoslovakia and Poland (1939). However, understanding that these developments led to World War II means evaluating how Hitler was able to gain traction politically during these years and why those who opposed him within and outside of Germany tolerated Nazi expansion before the outbreak of war.

The development of specific events or long-term trends is an outgrowth of human interests and motivations. This involves situating human affairs within the context of their immediate environment and their long-term tendencies. It does not absolve people of individual agency, but it helps explain the parameters of human behavior over time. For example, any discussion of Nazi Germany needs to consider the concepts of nationalism, anti-Semitism, fascism, and Marxism, all of which were important factors that influenced Hitler's ability to gain political support. In addition, circumstances over time allowed enough Germans to see Hitler's party as a viable alternative to the status quo.

History can show certain patterns that shape the way people interact with each other, though it does not mean that all people react the same way in similar situations. The search for conditions or contingencies can explain how people living in the same environment can respond to problems in different ways. It can also explain how people can become so dissatisfied with their current circumstances, or with other people, that they are willing to endorse or at least tolerate radical change or violence. In the case of Nazi Germany, conditions did not allow the Nazis to gain significant political support until the 1930s. Ongoing political malaise towards the Weimar Republic, heightened by the economic consequences of the Great Depression, gave the Nazi platform greater appeal to the German electorate.

The creation of Nazi Germany was not an inevitable outcome of these pressures, but it was the result of choices that people made in that moment. The development of a fascist state gave few legal options to oppose the entrenchment of the Nazi regime, allowing it to gain further support through its own success at revitalizing the German economy and its efforts at indoctrination through educational programs. The Germans had a long history of nationalism and anti-Semitism, which differed little from their neighbors, but only the Nazis transformed that persecution to the point of extermination. More than a decade of Nazi indoctrination that reframed racial attitudes toward the Jews, along with early war victories that allowed the Nazis to operate outside of the geographical boundaries of the German state, created conditions for the development of the Holocaust.

The pursuit of history as a type of sensemaking explains human actions within their own specific context and as part of broader trends. As a sensemaking activity, it also serves as a guide when applied to present circumstances. The key difference is that people are still in the process of making their decisions, making sense of their environment in real time.

History as a Guide to the Future: Learning From the Past

The ability to make sense of the past enables history to be a guide. History becomes a window into present circumstances and allows people to see how they reflect both the successes and failures of those who came before them. This general sentiment is captured in a cartoon published by Tom Toro in *Litro Magazine* (2012, June 25). It shows a historian talking to a psychiatrist with a caption that reads: "Those who don't study history are doomed to repeat it. Yet those who *do* study history are doomed to stand by helplessly while everyone else repeats it." This notion defines history as the study of human errors, as opposed to the study of human achievements, with the goal of improving the human condition by avoiding the mistakes of the past. It is better to view history as the study of human experiences, gauging how they handled the pressures that persist over time. These lessons can more easily be applied to the challenges people face today.

Linton and Vakil (2020) point out that the inherent weakness in sourcing strategies during the COVID pandemic resembles those of Japanese companies after the March 2011 earthquake in Fukushima, Japan. They published their observations with a sense of irony, remarking that "almost nine years later, it seems the lessons of Fukushima must be learned anew." In essence, history already shows that supply chain strategies were a problem. COVID simply highlighted that most companies did not learn from the past. That it was Japanese companies which experienced this most directly in 2011 should not matter. As John Lewis Gaddis (2008) remarks, history "can widen the range of experience beyond what we as individuals have encountered, if we can draw upon the experiences of others who've had to confront comparable situations in the past" (p. 9). History allows people to extend their search for guidance beyond family, friends, and co-workers.

Learning from the past requires the use of comparative history. Parallel experiences can provide clarity about current circumstances. This can be particularly relevant in difficult times. The Great Depression of the 1930s serves as an important case study on the development and impact of a financial crisis. It certainly influences the way western governments now engage in social welfare, from unemployment benefits to health care, serving as an example of a historical trend that extends to our current circumstances. The Great Depression also reveals how a financial crisis can affect all aspects of society. Even though most people did not invest in the stock market, the difficulties that began with the market crash in October 1929 had a ripple effect that led to unemployment and a further shrinking of the economy. Banks felt pressure from the market crash and their own customers, who either failed to make payments on their debts or tried to close their accounts. This, in turn, meant that banks did not have the cash reserves to provide short-term loans to companies, leading to further unemployment and continuing the cycle.

The lessons learned from the Great Depression influenced how the U.S. government responded to the recession of 2008. Congress quickly passed a bi-partisan economic stimulus bill aimed at stabilizing the banking industry in an effort to avoid a key factor that drove the global economy into its long depression of the 1930s. While this effort "saved the banks," allowing them to continue their role as lenders, it did not account for the individual borrowers who went into default on their mortgages due to unemployment. The resulting collapse of the housing market in 2009–2010 subsequently influenced the economic stimulus packages passed by the US government in 2020 as local and state governments issued shelter-in-place orders due to the COVID outbreak.

Historical comparisons require searching the past for similar circumstances or conditions to see how other people handled the same types of problems. The needs of the moment usually shape this search for guidance. The experience of dealing with COVID naturally produced comparisons with other global pandemics. The outbreak of influenza in 1917–1918 offers direct parallels to the pandemic of 2020 as there are similarities between each disease and the way many countries have tried to regulate public health. The relative success of combating the "Spanish flu" has been used to justify policies related to wearing masks, sheltering-in-place, restricting certain business activity, and limiting entertainment venues. Moreover, it serves to normalize the types of sacrifices that people across the globe experienced in 2020–2022 by demonstrating that such restrictions have been a normal reaction to the outbreak of disease.

Discovering similarities between past and present can also uncover patterns of behavior or attitudes that serve as corrections for today. This is where history can become the most controversial since the past can offer moral lessons. It is useful so long as communities share a common value system and are open to self-evaluation. It is easy to pass judgment on the Nazis because the Holocaust demonstrates that their values deviate greatly from what the bulk of humanity would consider moral. Very few people would consider Hitler to be anything other than an architect of evil. This, in turn, shapes the memory of World War II. Those who fought the Nazis are generally considered heroes, "the Greatest Generation," and are epitomized by the likes of Winston Churchill, Franklin Delano Roosevelt, and Dwight D. Eisenhower.

Moral judgments become murkier when people disagree on the way to apply them in today's setting. The American Civil War ultimately ended slavery in the United States, and like World War II, is remembered as a moral war. Contemporary efforts to remove public statues or war monuments dedicated to Confederate soldiers and their leaders have its roots in this memory of the past. Debates over what to do with imagery related to the Confederacy have less to do with ongoing support for the "Lost Cause" than it does with the way moral lessons from the past should be applied to the present. This type of debate speaks to the power of historical memory and the way that the past shapes identity.

History as Heritage

The use of history is often most meaningful when it touches upon people's core identity. History connects people to those who lived before and creates bonds between strangers who share a similar heritage. This is the core business strategy of Ancestry (ancestry.com) and other companies that specialize in genealogical services. Ancestry's marketing campaign centers on the importance of family and ethnic heritage as key components of a person's self-identity. Advertisements focus on DNA testing, which often demonstrates that many people have greater ethnic diversity in their family background than they realize. Highlighted individuals reveal that their experiences led them to a new sense of self-discovery that changed the way they think about themselves and the world. Such testing is only the beginning of the services that the company provides. Its genealogical branch offers people the ability to create significance from their family history. Ancestry initiated a campaign in 2019 that emphasized its role in collecting and sorting a myriad of archival resources based on a client's profile. Their goal was to make family history real, to offer documents and photographs which clients can use to piece together their family story. The company acts as an archivist and historian, selecting useful information and applying it to the criteria brought forward by their subscribers so that they can apply this information to the questions that led them to explore their family history in the first place.[4] In short, Ancestry learned how to market historical research.

History helps define a common heritage, serving as an anchor that holds people together. The "father" of western history, Herodotus, saw cultural bonds as a stronger marker of identity than either political allegiance or location. He viewed Greek identity as holding to a common religion, common ethnicity, common language, and common customs, applying these same rules to the myriad of other peoples that he introduced in his histories. Like the ancient Greeks, subsequent generations passed forward the ideas, customs, and institutions prevalent today. History clarifies essential attributes for organizational identities. As Marcus Collins and Peter Stearns (2020) remark:

> Group identity and history are inevitably intertwined. This is one reason that all modern nations encourage history being taught in schools: to provide a reasonably coherent narrative of the nation's development, its key events and institutions, and its (real or imagined) distinguishing characteristics. A sense of national identity provides a vital element of citizenship.
>
> (p. 22)

These remarks apply equally to non-political organizations as well. History can explain how an organization's heritage developed, along with its ongoing role as a focal point for unity. It can also isolate tensions that arise despite this common background and point out inconsistencies in the way members uphold an organization's stated values.

There is a close connection between shared values and traditions. Rituals or other practices that honor the past offer a way to participate in a common heritage with people across time. They have meaning because they reflect a heritage passed on through history. For example, Christians have practiced Communion, or the Eucharist, since the first century in imitation of the last meal that Jesus held with his disciples before his arrest and execution by the Roman government. It also reinforces the core message of Christian theology that claims Jesus died to forgive the sins of humanity. This reminds members of a church about the shared values that hold them together, not only as a local community but with others who adhere to the same beliefs across time and in other places.

National holidays serve a similar purpose, reminding people about the principles that hold a country together. They highlight those who founded, shaped, and protected the country from its inception. Flags are one of the most important symbols of national values. They have meaning because they are tied to the ideals that are rooted in the creation of each country. It is why people visit national monuments, like the Lincoln Memorial in Washington D.C. This works best alongside education in national history, where people learn about the country's past through foundational documents like the *Declaration of Independence*, the *U.S. Constitution*, and other texts that reflect the moral character of the country. This includes the study of important leaders who defended those values: certain presidents, civil rights leaders, and others who had a positive impact on implementing these ideals over time.

The idea of holding a common heritage is different than sameness. History traces how people create a sense of solidarity that adapts to new circumstances over time. The concept of heritage represents a type of continuity with the past that persists through change. Thus, it is possible to talk about being the same people as one's ancestors, even though each generation would feel out of place living in each other's environment. It also accounts for change, as a common heritage evolves over time, especially as communities get larger and more diverse.

The English priest Bede, who wrote *The Ecclesiastical History of the English People* in the 8th century for the Saxon King Ceowulf, offers an interesting look at the development of a common heritage amongst a diverse group of people. These include the Irish, Picts, Britons, Romans, Angles, and Saxons. The book features war and political intrigue between rulers who govern communities organized around their own ethnic heritages. Yet as Bede (1990) records events he frames them as conflicts between two basic groups of people: Christians and pagans. He also highlights the role of Romans, Britons, and the Irish in helping shape a new Christian identity for the Saxons. Bede's concluding entry summarizes his current setting in these terms:

At the present time, the Picts have a treaty of peace with the English, and are glad to be united in Catholic peace and truth to the universal Church. The Irish who are living in Britain are content with their own territories, and do not contemplate any raids or stratagems against the English. The Britons for the most part have a national hatred for the English, and uphold their own bad customs against the true Easter of the Catholic Church.

(p. 324)

Bede's depiction of Christianity as a force for peace between people in England underscores the importance of shared values in providing a sense of stability within communities and with their neighbors. Christianity would become the unifying heritage for the various people who would conquer and rule England in the future.

Every type of community operates with a set of beliefs or principles that shape their culture and guide their behavior, whether it is a family, neighborhood, country, religious organization, non-profit, or business. History uses previous settings as case studies that show how well people generally uphold the values that define their communities. History can also diagnose where and how a breakdown in values occur in practice. This can help explain the development of current problems. For the Roman historian Livy, who lived through an age of civil war and political change at the advent of the first century, the transformation of Rome into an Empire was a necessary corrective to the moral decay of the Roman Republic. The loss of traditional shared values meant that the Romans could "neither endure our vices nor face the remedies needed to cure them" (Livy, 2002, p. 30). Livy was speaking to a contemporary audience, primarily the educated elite, to justify that political change had restored the values they had lost under the Republic. His audience clearly understood the problems they faced, but Livy wanted to reframe the discussion around the shared values that defined being Roman against the process of change over time. He was making an argument about continuity through change. This was the key for Caesar Augustus to bring radical organizational change to Rome and usher in a period of unprecedented peace.

Leaders Should Be Historically Minded

It should be evident by now that history can be used for a variety of purposes. It is a way of thinking about the past and its constant influence on the future.[5] Historians do not simply write history for others to consume. They *teach* history so that others can pursue the past as well. This isn't simply an exercise that takes place in a classroom. Historical writing at its best introduces the goals, methodology, and resources used in a study, followed by a discussion that illustrates how these sources build historical understanding. Historians want others to see what they see in the past. Ultimately the reader is responsible for carrying forward this teaching into their own lives.

The intellectual skills associated with history, and the information derived from historical research, are accessible to anyone who chooses to pursue them. Patrick Murphy and Ray Coye (2013) decided to turn to history to help explain internal divisions within corporate leadership teams. Neither had advanced training in historical methodology before deciding to study mutiny in the Age of Discovery as a parallel to this contemporary problem. They went all in and learned how to conduct historical research from primary sources so that they could know first-hand how problems of mutiny developed on ships that made voyages of exploration in the 16th and 17th centuries. They examined four case studies centered around individual captains who experienced mutinies against their authority. This allowed them to test for common experiences (continuities) within different settings (contingencies). What they discovered was a set of common factors that are also applicable to the contingencies associated with modern organizations. They concluded, no matter the setting, that internal threats developed because leaders and the rest of the organization did not share the same values at the time of insurrection. Even though the specific values associated with those sea voyages and today's organizations differ, "this difference is in content, not functions. The mechanisms by which values are shared by members and violated by leaders are still the same" (p. 156). One of the key takeaways from the book is that stable leadership requires adhering to the values that form the basis of relationships between people within any organization.

Leaders should develop a historical mindset so that the advantages derived from history can be easily employed. This does not mean that leaders need to pursue academic research. History is an intellectual resource that can be used alongside other metrics when evaluating an organization, its people, and its goals. This was the central focus of a round table discussion published by the *Harvard Business Review* in 1986. The participants emphasized the importance of history for business managers, introducing a variety of ways that pursing history strengthened business decisions. Among the highlights are history's emphasis on case studies, its concern for contextualizing problems, its application of comparative methodology, and its role as an anchor for collective memory. The discussion further stresses the need to teach emerging business leaders the complexity of the world and its relationship to the past. Thomas McCraw summarizes the group's general perspective:

we all agree that history is a way of thinking – a way of searching for patterns and trying to see if such patterns recur from one situation to another. It helps us think about the parameters of what's possible, what the boundaries of likely action or possible success are.

(Kantrow, 1986, p. 82)

Their advice is not limited to the history of leadership. They encourage leaders to study history more broadly to better situate their companies for success.

John Seaman and George Smith (2012), in their *Harvard Business Review Article* titled "Your Company's History as a Leadership Tool," argue that the historian's craft is a valuable tool when leaders are engaged in change management. They note that historical thinking "requires an appreciation of the dynamic nature of change in a complex human system. It demands an understanding of the particularity of problems and the often unintended consequences of their solutions" (p. 50). This mindset places organizational change within the context of larger trajectories. It also requires the discovery and use of an organization's past. A historical mindset presents a realistic look at the development of current problems, making sense of recent challenges by tracing their origins or discovering parallel examples from the past. History places adversity into context and offers ways to handle new circumstances when they arise. It also produces a sense of identity and purpose that can inspire people to persevere through change. The past reflects the values shared by those invested in an organization, establishing unchanging principles that serve as an anchor when new directions are needed.

Seaman and Smith (2012) offer ways that leaders can develop historical mindsets that are specific to their organizations. It can start simply with a survey of company records. They suggest visiting the company archives and adding to its material interviews from long-tenured employees and departing executives. These can add depth to the written record and fill in gaps not recorded in the company's documentation. The next step is to engage the broader organization about the company' history and values. A survey of employees can offer additional information, but more importantly, it can reveal how the company's history shapes current perceptions about the organization. Leadership can then engage in a dialogue about the meaning of the company's past with those within and outside the organization. It is important to be transparent about the company's past. This means making the people, products, and brands that form the organization's history accessible. Furthermore, they present several ways to make history an ongoing part of company practices. One is to review major projects at their conclusion to learn from the successes and failures of those processes. They also suggest taking a historical perspective before making major decisions: new strategies, marketing campaigns, acquisitions, or investments. Finally, leadership should make history part of ongoing conversations. This includes the celebration of current achievements and the memorialization of important developments for the future of the company.

Embracing history means taking a contextual view of an organization and its people. This requires evaluating current goals and practices as a historian looks at the way past leaders managed responsibilities. As Martin Gutmann (2018) proposes, it means being aware of the larger social, economic, and environmental structures that condition leadership decisions. Company records must be seen in context, not simply as a reflection of the way an organization conducts business at a certain time, but in relationship to the people responsible for its operation and those it serves. Customers and employees belong to many human organizations: families, social networks, educational institutions, cities, countries, religious institutions, charities, etc. This gives them multiple identities and allegiances that can shift over time. Understanding relationships between multiple organizations and those they mutually serve can matter too.

The Ford Motor Company serves as a useful example to illustrate the benefits of a historical mindset as part of business strategy.[6] It is a forward-looking organization. Its past represents a legacy of innovation and service, documented on its website through a company timeline of important achievements. At the same time, the company's heritage is placed within the context of significant events that allow the organization to highlight its values and its relationship to the larger community.

The company embraces the organization's history as a central feature of its identity and purpose:

> Henry Ford transformed not only the automobile but working life and the role of transportation. Having played our part in everything from the birth of the middle class to the recent global pandemic, we serve the world with integrity and competence. The Blue Oval is one of the most recognized corporate symbols in history, continually striving to earn the trust of all stakeholders.

Ford naturally highlights the positive contributions made by its founder and his successors, emphasizing the company's innovations and philanthropy. History takes the role of demonstrating continuity through change. It shows how the company's current and future practices reflect what it has always been even as it adapts to new circumstances. The Ford Motor Company links its goals to the past, choosing those parts of its history that reflect its positive values as a statement of who they are now and what they choose to aim for in the future.

Corporate leadership decided to frame their decision to produce ventilators to assist with the fight against COVID-19 alongside the company's role in assisting the U.S. government to procure military vehicles during World War II and its investment in medical technology to help the civilian population.

This places corporate decisions within the larger environment that shaped the American population during the 1940s. It also ties technological innovations to community needs. The first example, the production of a portable incubator to assist in the survival of premature infants, highlights Henry Ford's concern for infant mortality and creating an inexpensive devise that could be used in rural communities. This story celebrates compassion, innovation, and service to those in need. The second example, improvements to a portable lung to help with the Polio crisis of the late 1940s, ties the company to an earlier health crisis. This serves as a transition to Ford's recent partnership with 3M and GE Healthcare to produce supplies in the fight against the newer health crisis against COVID. The company's history makes sense of recent manufacturing decisions while also displaying a consistent value system.

These stories reflect important moments in the history of the Ford Motor Company. They demonstrate the company's commitment to innovation, though they stand out because they reflect parallel circumstances to the general issues faced across the globe in 2020–2021. These connections are an important part of the organization's public image. The company's history is under the stewardship of their head archivist, the historian Ted Ryan, who joined Ford in 2018 after spending 21 years as the image historian at Coca-Cola. He describes his role:

> What I do is organize, disseminate and preserve the history of a corporation. . . . At its core, we [archives] preserve the materials to tell the story of the corporation, automobiles, the brand. We preserve those for the future with an eye toward activating the materials in a meaningful way that helps the business.
>
> (Howard, 2018)

Ford's role in developing and producing medical devices during times of need has always reflected part of the organization's commitment to its community. Recent emphasis on this tradition is particularly meaningful in light of COVID. It reinforces the company's broader purpose: "to help build a better world, where every person is free to move and pursue their dreams." It also connects the company to the experiences of ordinary people by offering services outside of its loyal customer base. This works because it shows a pattern that places the company and its operations within the context of human struggles and triumphs.

Conclusion

Leaders who develop a historical mindset are better equipped to leverage the past in their approach to leadership. Many decisions are rooted in the ability to think temporally. History offers a way to evaluate continuity and change, but more importantly, it can help identify the boundaries that shape the way leaders can make effective change. It provides a cultural awareness that can promote meaningful and relevant organizational identity, loyalty, and pride. It also establishes nuanced perspectives on current trends that can help establish short-term and long-term trajectories for future planning. Moreover, history offers a sense of comparison that helps situate an organization's strengths and weaknesses. It provides context to organizational practices, helping determine core functions and those best suited for specific settings, some of which may have changed or no longer exist.

The next chapter introduces key aspects of the Renaissance, Enlightenment, and Industrial Revolution to illustrate some of the characteristics of history outlined in this chapter. These represent movements that help define their eras and lay the foundation for much of contemporary history. They also offer recognizable historical markers that serve as useful starting points to demonstrate continuity and change, while making it easier to draw comparisons between these eras and today. Chapter two ultimately functions as a primer for later chapters in this book. It contextualizes the relationship between people, leaders, and organizations that mattered within these historical periods. More importantly, it demonstrates timeless characteristics of effective leadership and lessons that apply as much today as they did in the past.

Notes

1. Primary resources are documents and other sources that were produced by the people being studied.
2. Historiography is the philosophy and methods of historical writing.
3. Vigorous debates on the nature of history extends back to ancient historians. Marwick (2001), Lukacs (2012), and Hewitson (2014) offer a good representation of recent trends.
4. Ancestry (2019) *Bringing Your Backstory to Life*
5. Staley (2006) goes so far to argue that "the historian's method for representing the past is an excellent method for representing the future" (p. 2).
6. The information used here on the Fort Motor Company was retrieved from its corporate website (Ford, *Our History*, corporate.ford.com)

References

Bede. (1990). *The ecclesiastical history of the English people*. Penguin Books.
Burns, J. M. (1978). *Leadership*. Harper Perennial.
Carr, E. H. (1961). *What is history?* Vintage Books.
Collins, M., & Stearns, P. (2020). *Why study history?* London Publishing Partnership.

Dalrymple, W. (2019). *The anarchy: The East India Company, corporate violence, and the pillage of an empire*. Bloomsbury.

Erikson, E. (2014). *Between monopoly and free trade: The English East India Company, 1600–1757*. Princeton University Press.

Gaddis, J. L. (2008). *The landscape of history: How historians map the past*. Oxford University Press.

Goodwin, D. K. (2018). *Leadership: In turbulent times*. Simon & Schuster.

Gutmann, M. (2018). Consulting the past: Integrating historians into history-based leadership studies. *Journal of Leadership Studies, 12*(2), 35–39.

Henry of Huntingdon (2002). *The history of the English people 1000–1154* (D. Greenway, Ed. & Trans.). Oxford University Press.

Hewitson, M. (2014). *History and causality*. Palgrave Macmillan.

Howard, P. (2018, July 29). *Historian swore he'd never leave Coca-Cola – then Ford called*. Detroit Free Press.

Ianziti, G. (2012). *Writing history in Renaissance Italy: Leonardo Bruni and the uses of the past*. Harvard University Press.

Kantrow, Alan M. (1986, January). Why history matters to managers. *Harvard Business Review, 64*, 81–89.

Koehn, N. (2017). *Forged in crisis: The power of courageous leadership in turbulent times*. Simon & Schuster.

Linton, T., & Vakil, B. (2020, March 5). *Coronavirus is proving we need more resilient supply chains*. Harvard Business Review. https://hbr.org/2020/03/coronavirus-is-proving-that-we-need-more-resilient-supply-chains

Livy. (2002). *The early history of Rome*. Penguin Books.

Lukacs, J. (2012). *The future of history*. Yale University Press.

Marwick, A. (2001). *The new nature of history: Knowledge, evidence, language*. Oxford University Press.

Murphy, P. J., & Coye, R. W. (2013). *Mutiny and its bounty*. Yale University Press.

National Commission on Terrorist Attacks Upon the United States (2004). *The 9/11 commission report*. W. W. Norton & Company.

Seaman Jr., J. T., & Smith, G. D. (2012, December). *Your company's history as a leadership tool*. Harvard Business Review.

Staley, D. J. (2006.) *History and future: Using historical thinking to imagine the future*. Lexington Books.

Tey, J. (1951). *The daughter of time*. Simon & Schuster.

Toro, Tom. (2012, June 25). *Those who don't study history*. [cartoon] Litro Magazine.

2 The Renaissance, Enlightenment, and Industrial Revolution

Introduction

History is an expository discipline that offers a repertoire of knowledge that can be applied to any situation. Making use of this knowledge requires a general understanding of the past and its significance. This chapter uses examples from the Renaissance (ca. 1350–1600), Enlightenment (ca. 1688–1800), and Industrial Revolution (ca. 1770–1840) to illustrate some of the characteristics of good history outlined in chapter one. These are historical frameworks that generalize important trends in western history. They represent movements that produced cultural and institutional change within their own settings and are commonly associated with the broader political, religious, and economic transformations that form the basis of modern society. While it is easy to see that life is much different today than it was in 1820, let alone the 1400s, the experiences of those who lived through these earlier times established much of what is taken for granted today.

The following discussion can only offer highlights from this four-hundred-year timespan. It emphasizes aspects of each movement that align with the book's focus on organizational leadership. The primary goal is to condition the reader towards a historical mindset that will be applied throughout the remainder of the book. Developing a historical mindset does not require professional training. It does rely on the ability to sift through many variables to identify the most important factors that matter in any given moment. Good history leads to nuanced evaluations of interpersonal relationships and external conditions that influence new ideas or actions. This requires a detailed exposition on the factors that shape the way people respond to each other and their environment. Historical trends reveal the variable or variables that influence people in multiple settings across time.

The Renaissance, Enlightenment, and Industrial Revolution were chosen because they have recognizable historical markers that build off each other and resonate with the way organizations exist today. They provide good

DOI: 10.4324/9781003100171-2

starting points to illustrate how history unpacks the complexities that shape human developments over time, especially the way historians contextualize trends and explain their ongoing significance. Each section contains case studies that are situated as part of a larger overview of each movement, emphasizing history's role in identifying patterns that account for continuity and change, some of which still drive human interaction. This applies to developments within this timespan, such as the influence of the Renaissance on the Enlightenment, as well as the long-lasting imprint of these movements.

The Renaissance

The Renaissance was an intellectual and cultural movement that has come to define a period of historical change (ca. 1350–ca.1600), serving as a bridge from the medieval to modern eras. Historians of the mid-19th century defined this as a type of cultural rebirth that placed western civilization on a path toward modernity. They recognized that their own society was rooted in certain trends that developed during the 15th and 16th centuries. Jacob Burckhardt (1860/1990), the most recognized of these historians, argued that Italy's decentralized political environment and its commitment to a culture of humanism pushed Europe beyond medieval culture. Italians represented the value of individual achievement, refined through an education shaped by antiquity, and reinforced through the production of artwork, architecture, and written texts. Moreover, he viewed the Renaissance as a more secular age, departing from the religious influences that characterized the medieval past.

Most historians have significantly modified Burkhardt's conclusions.[1] Much of what he identified as the legacy of the Renaissance was filtered through the secularization of the Enlightenment. Yet the Renaissance was a period of change, and Burkhardt's narrative on the relationship between politics, humanism, and culture still resonates. This did not lead to a unified movement of artistic achievement and reform. The Renaissance is defined as much as by global exploration, religious reform, and royal expansion as it is by the experiences of Italian city-states. However, the spread of humanism across Europe did create a more educated society and expanded the number of people capable of resolving contemporary problems. Humanism took many forms and was adapted to meet various challenges during this period. It also set a trajectory that links education, social mobility, and leadership that is still relevant in the 21st century.

The Renaissance does not have a definitive beginning or end. It evolved from trends that characterized the late medieval period and would gradually transform into the early Enlightenment. Humanists of the 16th century looked back to the mid-14th century as a starting point because they identified several literary authors as precursors to their movement. The examples given below represent some of the factors that contributed to the development of humanism, its impact on civic leadership, and its adaptation by the church. This gives only a partial picture of the Renaissance, but it demonstrates the importance of humanism, its significance to organizational change, and aspects of effective leadership that continue to be relevant.

Development of Humanism

Humanism or *studia humanitatis* was an educational model based on the study of ancient texts. It emphasized a well-rounded education that applied not only to the elite but also to the craftsmen and journeymen who produced the artwork cherished by the patrons who employed them. Imitating the classical style in art and architecture reinforced humanist principles for public consumption. This did not replace Christianity. However, it emphasized human achievements and taught that the knowledge contained in non-Christian texts held equal authority when managing secular affairs. This education proliferated first in northern Italy, providing the intellectual skills necessary to raise the status of merchants as diplomats and statesmen. It led to social mobility within cities, elevating new groups of people into positions of influence within secular and religious institutions.

This practice evolved from a long tradition of using ancient knowledge within the medieval church. Monasteries had been tasked with preserving ancient texts since the early Middle Ages. Their libraries offered some of the first manuscripts consulted by the humanists of the 14th century. The institutionalization of the church in the 12th and 13th centuries offered a more standard use of ancient knowledge. Italian universities trained clergy in Roman law; medieval philosophers began employing ancient philosophy in a dialectic with Roman theologians to seek clarification on Biblical truth. The goal was to harmonize theology with classical philosophy, particularly Aristotle and the Neoplatonist philosophers of late-antiquity (4th–7th centuries). These efforts significantly expanded the church's role in medieval life, preparing many clerics for careers in bureaucracy and law.

Francesco Petrarch, a Florentine cleric whose career was tied to the papal court at Avignon during the mid-14th century, is an important bridge between the use of classical knowledge within the church and popular efforts to emulate the classical style in poetry. Petrarch was the product of a university education steeped in Roman knowledge, using his career as a diplomat for the papal court to visit local libraries and establish a broad literary circle. He was particularly interested in the reconstruction of ancient texts, contributing to the development of textual criticism, a technique to determine the original version of a text from later variant copies. His writings imitated classical styles and themes, which largely pertained to human affairs rather than theology. His poetry reflected the passions of life, and his sonnets became a standard for later poets.

Petrarch was not unique in imitating the Roman style or writing in the vernacular. What stands out is the way he engaged with the classical past to make it meaningful. He addressed a series of letters to classical authors that presumed their interest in the future. They were, in fact, written to his peers and appealed to ancient people as having contemporary relevance. This connection between past and present placed events in Europe as part of a long continuum that began with the Roman Empire. Petrarch was particularly motivated by what he considered to be growing corruption in the church and its impact on political stability within Europe. His letters addressed notions of identity, connecting his present time not only with the ancient fathers of the church but also with the non-Christian founders of European culture. Thus, humanism first developed within the context of ecclesiastical change and the secular pursuits of clergy.

Humanism has its roots in the growing wealth and status of Italian merchants, whose economic and political roles in the 14th and 15th centuries placed them in a position to grow the humanist movement. Italians had long served as intermediaries between the eastern Mediterranean and western Europe. By 1300 they dominated trade to China through the Black Sea, which gave access to a unified trade route established by the Mongols. In addition to trade, they offered transport to pilgrims and crusaders and served as a source of knowledge about foreign cultures. The role of Italian bankers, who began financing European warfare in the 14th century, gave some cities a more prominent role in diplomacy. This became particularly important during the Hundred Years War (1337–1453) between England and France.

Italians were also invested in warfare against the Ottoman Empire in the Eastern Mediterranean. Italian cities frequently supported the later crusades, which brought them into alliances with the Byzantine Empire.[2] This gave Italian merchants access to teachers and texts that were less accessible to other Europeans. Greek diplomats and refugees would sometimes find work as translators and teachers as they sought aid from Italian cities against Ottoman expansion. Manuel Chrysoloras, who served as an ambassador from the Byzantine Empire in 1394, helped establish the first humanist school in Florence. This gave Italian cities access to a repository of ancient Greek knowledge that had been lost to medieval scholars.

The first humanist schools were developed in the late 14th century to teach children from wealthy merchant families to be good citizens and serve their city's interests, particularly the mercantile Republics of Florence, Genoa, and Venice. Mark Jurdjevic (1999) comments that the goal was to emulate the "Ciceronian exaltation of civil life" (p. 1000). This concept emphasized that the best leaders were scholar-statements who used their wealth to invest in their communities. Those who pursued and maintained this education considered themselves humanists, dedicated to the humanities, the basis of a liberal arts education that could allow an individual to adapt their knowledge and skills to a variety of settings. The study of grammar, logic, and rhetoric was intended to prepare for a life of persuasion and diplomacy. Arithmetic, geometry, and astronomy were central to navigation and architecture. Literature, history, and moral philosophy were the basis of virtue and ethics.

Italian humanism would have a significant impact on the nature of leadership during the Renaissance. It taught that public leaders should be guided by the principle of *virtù*. This term had a flexible meaning. Sometimes it was used to reflect moral virtue, especially among the earlier humanists. Other times the term represented a leader's innate capabilities. Niccolò Machiavelli (1532/1998) separated *virtù* from morality, representing a leader's "excellence" rather than ethics. Few humanists made such a stringent distinction. Baldassare Castiglione's *The Book of the Courtier* (1528/1976), written in the form of a Platonic dialogue, was essentially a handbook on etiquette and manners for men and women who wished to serve in royal or princely courts. It taught merchants to behave with civility and established the humanities – history, literature, poetry, philosophy, music, art theory – as a reservoir of shared knowledge that was meaningful in a court setting.

This value of this education spread through personal interaction, first within Italian cities, then to other areas visited by merchants and diplomats. Brian Maxon (2014) emphasizes the importance of learned connections, noting that they allowed people to build relationships with those of a higher status. He notes that "courtiers abroad with knowledge of classical rhetoric possessed an advantage in courts where the ruler sought to project the appearance of being a friend to humanists." Humanism also became a way for people to build social and economic circles. "Sharing humanist interests brought kinsmen together in branches of families. They drew people together for business deals and marriages" (pp. 38–39). Investment in public education, art, and building projects extended these connections to the larger community. Humanism became a means of connecting with people to advance a person's career or provide a better life for a person's family.

Civic Leadership in Renaissance Italy

Humanists generally expected that an education in the classics would equip people to become better leaders. They taught that good leadership was based on common values and was best expressed through reciprocal relationships.

These ideals were implemented within the context of larger political dynamics. Humanism shaped leaders, who leveraged their education to establish their influence, and then sponsored a broader humanist culture to facilitate socio-political stability. The interplay between politics and culture led to humanism's broader impact throughout Europe.

The Medici family serves as a quintessential model for this development. They are traditionally credited with transforming Florence into a center of Renaissance culture by sponsoring humanist scholars and extending their patronage to the arts. Humanism certainly contributed to their success, though this went alongside their more traditional roles as part of the city's elite. The Medici built their wealth in the cloth industry, originating in the countryside before moving into the city at the end of the 13th century, expanding their business to include shipping companies and an international bank. Their influence rested on their capacity to establish and maintain social and economic relationships through a complex system of patronage. By the end of the 14th century, they became particularly influential among the newer families in the city who had immigrated in the aftermath of the Black Death (1347–1351).

Cosimo de Medici emerged as the city's most influential leader after a popular coup against the ruling oligarchy in 1434. He was one of the only leading figures to oppose Florence's disastrous military campaign against the city of Lucca in 1433. This event was the catalyst to Medici power and Florence's transformation into a cultural center for humanism. However, this circumstance must be placed within the context of the family's long relationship with the city's various factions. Gene Brucker (1957) traces three important elements that defined social standing in Florence during the 14th century: family connections, wealth, and political representation. He argues that Cosimo benefited from two divergent trends, the family's standing as political outsiders after the Ciompi Revolt (1378) and the economic connections developed after the creation of the Medici bank in 1397. Padgett and Ansell (1993) argue that Cosimo inherited a broad coalition of support from his father Giovanni that represented overlapping marriage, economic, and other social ties. Cosimo represented the only source of unity for the various merchants, craftsmen, and other residents who rebelled against the city's rulers.

Cosimo's authority derived from his social and political influence rather than control of the government. In his youth, Cosimo had been part of a burgeoning circle of humanist scholars, the first to be educated by the new humanist schools in the city. He was a pupil to Roberto Rossi, a wealthy patrician turned humanist, who introduced Cosimo to the works of Cicero and Livy. This motivated Cosimo to build a private collection of classical books. Rossi was the first humanist scholar to benefit from Cosimo's patronage, receiving funds to travel and copy classical literature for the development of the Medici library. Cosimo also entered the intellectual circle of Niccolò Niccolli, another Florentine patrician who sponsored a community of scholars, whose collection of more than 800 classical books was funded in part by loans from the Medici bank. Cosimo integrated this collection into his patronage of the church of San Marco to become the first public library in Florence. This was one of the ways that humanism became accessible to the broader community.

At the same time, Cosimo's influence depended on his effectiveness as a civic leader. He established a self-sacrificing reputation by using the bank to cover shortfalls in city revenues and to provide support for the refurbishment of the city. The bank also served as a vehicle for international diplomacy. Medici funding allowed for the continuation of a church council organized by Pope Eugenius IV at Ferrara, with the condition that it would be transferred to Florence. The subsequent Council of Florence (1439) became an important symbol of Medici status in the city. Cosimo enshrined his role as patron of the council in his private chapel, commissioning the artist Benozzo Gozzoli to use it as inspiration for the mural *Journey of the Magi* in 1459. The economic relationships created through the bank's various Italian branches helped Cosimo negotiate peace between Milan and Venice, ending a series of wars that had dominated northern Italy during the first half of the 15th century.

International diplomacy allowed Cosimo to showcase his effectiveness as a leader, and by extension the benefits of a humanist education. Patronage of public and private buildings enabled him to connect more broadly with the population of Florence. This was most evident in the reconstruction and refurbishment of churches. The Renaissance style echoed the Roman past, in part, because the earliest churches were founded in the 4th and 5th centuries and were in desperate need of repair. The desire for unity and symmetry meant that newer churches were refurbished in the classical style. Dale Kent (2000) observes that these buildings allowed Cosimo to enthusiastically teach humanism to a more popular audience. Public libraries and artwork were often attached to these construction projects. Kent highlights Cosimo's support for the confraternity of Santo Martino, which in turn sponsored public performances of poetry and songs in the classical style. This gave artisans the opportunity to participate in humanist culture. These types of connections allowed the Medici to become the center of this cultural movement.

The Medici are significant because they adapted humanism as a sociopolitical tool and modeled its use. By the end of the 15th century, artistic and literary patronage had become a regular function of civic leadership throughout Italy. These served as identity markers that reflected shared values between leaders and their communities. Such patronage did not necessarily extend to the political ideals of republicanism endorsed by many humanists. Martines (2003) argues that Lorenzo de Medici, Cosimo's grandson, was able to leverage his role as a patron of the arts and an international peacemaker to consolidate his authority over the Florentine government. His effectiveness as a leader and his support for a common humanist culture was more important than maintaining the city's traditional political institutions.

The ability to use humanism as a source of cultural unity was adapted by a variety of leaders. Florentine artists received commissions from rulers throughout northern Italy seeking to fulfill their duties as patrons. The artist and inventor Leonardo da Vinci completed some of his more famous works for Ludovico Sforza, duke of Milan, whose father had conquered the city from the Visconti family. The mural painting *The Last Supper* is perhaps the most recognizable of Da Vinci's commissioned pieces for the Sforza family. He was also responsible for designing theatrical productions and court festivities that emphasized Ludovico's relationship with Milan.

Most of Europe had adopted some elements of humanism by the early 16th century. The invention of the moveable type printing press in the 1440s expanded access to the classical texts and commentaries at the heart of a humanist education. This allowed these texts to become accessible to a growing demographic of 'middle-class' professionals. Nobles and civic leaders learned the value of classical rhetoric from Italian merchants and diplomats. This prompted monarchs like Francis I of France and Henry VIII of England to foster a culture of learning that elevated the role of education among their counselors and transformed the function of their courts.

Humanism and the Church

Humanism facilitated changes within the church. Artistic patronage became a way to rebuild churches and make new connections with local congregations. Humanism more broadly influenced the way theologians and philosophers approached Christian teachings. It also sharpened theological debates and added new participants to religious reform.

The church's commitment to humanism must be placed within the context of its need to reestablish its credibility. The papacy had long received criticism that it abused its authority through secular pursuits. In the 13th century, this applied to the use of crusading against those who would challenge its authority over the papal states in central Italy. Criticism became more pronounced in the 14th century after the popes moved to the city of Avignon. Petrarch argued that the popes belonged in Rome. Their decision to remain in a foreign city abandoned their duty as the head of the church and facilitated further corruption. Gregory IX's decision to return to Rome in 1378 failed to resolve this issue. Cardinals and their secular allies had become so divided that it led to a period of papal schism, with two and sometimes three popes claiming authority over the church. Trust in papal leadership was at an all-time low by the time a resolution was reached at the Council of Constance in 1417.

By the middle of the 15th century, the papacy viewed patronage as a central part of its effort to revitalize the church and restore Rome as the global capital of Christianity. They were influenced by the Medici family's success at using humanism to build trust within Florence and establish peace with the city's neighbors. Nicholas V, the first humanist pope, established the Vatican library in 1451 to solidify Rome's position as the center of Christian learning. These plans were carried forward by Pope Sixtus IV, who greatly expanded his predecessor's collection and turned it into a public library. Sixtus also sought to transform papal sponsorship of humanism into a building program that would reinforce his own status as the head of the Roman church. This included his role as the ruler of the papal states. The construction of the Sistine Chapel and the Ponte Sixto, the first new bridge in Rome since ancient times, were the most important building projects of his pontificate. These efforts firmly established support for humanism as an essential feature of papal leadership. Pope Julius II made it central to his management of Rome after becoming pope in 1503. It fulfilled his obligations as the ecclesiastical sovereign of the city and represented his personal tastes as a patron.[3]

Humanism reshaped papal leadership by bringing it into alignment with the way civic leaders reinforced their authority. Yet humanism also prompted an effort to restore the church to an earlier model of ecclesiastical life that contrasted with cultural expectations in Italy. For example, Erasmus used his satire *Julius Excluded from Heaven* (Erasmus, 1989, pp. 142–173) in 1514 to highlight discrepancies between the model of leadership offered by Renaissance popes and those of the early church, a continuation of arguments made by Petrarch in the 14th century. The book was written in the form of a dialogue between the recently deceased Pope Julius II and Saint Peter, regarded as the first pope, who guards the gates to Heaven and refused to let Julius for living a secular rather than religious life. The comedic interplay between the two represents a scathing attack on the head of the church, exposing corruption through humor. The goal was to encourage the use of humanism to reform papal leadership.

The Protestant Reformation grew out of this dynamic. Martin Luther's theological challenges against the use of indulgences in the *95 Theses* (1517) were not far from the criticisms leveled by other humanists like Erasmus. Luther wanted a rhetorical debate, in public, to place pressure on church authorities to change their practices. This discussion quickly shifted to the nature of papal authority over the church. These debates took place in print and in person to an educated audience of clergy and laity. The spread of humanist education in northern Europe, which emphasized rhetoric, logic, and the use of classical texts, including scripture, had enough resonance that the secular elite could engage in making decisions about the issue. Political support from the dukes of Saxony allowed Luther to develop his ideas and reorganize the churches of northern Germany outside of the Roman system.

Reform of the Genevan church came closest toward integrating humanist ideals within an ecclesiastical system. John Calvin was a second-generation reformer, trained in theology and philosophy at the University of Paris. He was a humanist scholar; his first publication in 1532 was a commentary on Seneca's *De Clementia*, a Roman philosophical essay evaluating the relationship between rulers and their subjects. William Bouwsma (1990) remarks that humanism shaped Calvin's ideas in two fundamental ways. First was his reverence for the Christian past, particularly for what he referred to as the "primitive church." The second was his reliance on rhetoric as an instrument of reform. Calvin was a student of the past, not just the early church, but his own contemporary history. After making the decision to break with the Roman church, Calvin opted to leave France in self-imposed exile to the Swiss Confederation. The Holy Roman Empire had bitterly divided over Protestant reform, and Calvin did not want to bring civil war to his home country. He wanted to convince the French monarchy to support Protestant reform, using rhetoric to appeal to King Francis I, himself a strong supporter of humanism.

Calvinism developed within the context of the broader religious and political changes taking place in the Swiss Confederation.[4] Geneva was in the process of becoming a Protestant community when Calvin arrived, but its inhabitants were deeply divided, so the city council sought outside help to deal with their own factionalism. Calvin was concerned that church practices and Christian conduct conform to the values of scripture. His reforms were based on the notion that the citizens of Geneva and the Christian community were one and the same. At the same time, the city also used religious reform as the foundation for a new independent government. The dukes of Savoy had controlled Geneva through its bishop. The establishment of a Protestant church rejected foreign religious and political authority. The biggest challenge was creating a system that reflected the essence of early Christianity while adapting to Geneva's civic culture.

The *Ecclesiastical Ordinances* (1541), which defined the offices and function of the church, were tied to the creation of the Republic of Geneva. Calvin developed a leadership structure for the church that reflected the spiritual equality of all its members and ensured the cooperation of church and state. The Company of Pastors was responsible for overseeing doctrine and pastoral training. It granted the city government some input into the men selected for pastoral leadership while reserving quality control to the pastors themselves. Members of the laity served in positions of leadership as elders, who were jointly responsible with the pastors for church discipline. Representatives among the pastors and elders served on the Consistory, the disciplinary body of the church. This allowed all parties a role in church leadership while giving those with ecclesiastical training the authority to safeguard Christian teaching.

Calvinism became the model for religious reform in southern France, the Netherlands, and Scotland. Calvin had hoped to craft an organization that would maintain the unity of the church. Instead, he created a system that could be adapted by different communities, which would have an ongoing impact on Christianity for centuries.

These examples captured the essence of the Renaissance as a whole. Humanism offered a consistent method of leadership that was applied differently among a variety of organizations and institutions. Its influence was based on the integration of humanist learning, cultural trends, and larger geopolitical interests. Humanism was a catalyst for historical change during the Renaissance, a common influence on the people who shaped this era.

The Enlightenment

The Enlightenment was a self-defined intellectual and cultural movement during the 18th century that grew out of the political and religious tensions that developed during the Renaissance. Philosophes, the well-rounded philosophers of the Enlightenment, read classical texts but viewed them as inherently flawed. They continued to believe that shared values were the key to cultural stability. However, they advocated a break from previous traditions. Philosophes emphasized the use of human reason rather than classical knowledge as the source for change. They sought to understand humanity as part of the natural world, outside of the cultural variations inherent in each society and viewed the ancients with as much skepticism as they did later authorities. Their goal was to work toward a universal understanding of human nature that could provide a bridge between different cultures and bring peace.

Historians view the 18th century as a period of transition that provided the foundation for modern thought. Philosophes tended to provide theoretical solutions to contemporary problems, providing the intellectual foundation for organizational change. Many of these concepts are still relevant. Notions of progress, human achievement, human equality, political liberty, and economic freedom are among the many ideas that have shaped western culture and influenced the rest of the world.

These ideas were meant to resolve a variety of problems that had emerged by the 17th century. There are more factors than can be accounted for here. Ultimately it was the way traditional authorities responded to ongoing conflicts that prompted this new intellectual movement. One of the most important trends was the development of absolutism, which became the dominant political system in Europe during the 18th century. Like those in Renaissance, intellectual leaders during the Enlightenment viewed government as a relationship between rulers and people that was based on a shared identity and common values. Absolutism rewrote this relationship by using the monarch as basis for cultural solidarity. The following discussion introduces absolutism as an important catalyst to the Enlightenment. Debates over government and its role in society gave the Enlightenment greater influence and established public discourse as an important vehicle for organizational change.

Development of Absolutism

The term "absolutism" was created in the 19th century to represent a sociopolitical system that uses identity and culture to reinforce a monarch's authority. Most European governments reflected at least some attributes of absolutism during the 18th century. The theoretical justification of this system was not new. Monarchs represented God's divine authority over government, a concept that went back to the Middle Ages. However, this authority now applied to the whole kingdom without recourse to other local or regional leaders. Yet absolutism did not mean that a monarch wielded arbitrary power. King Louis XIV of France, who established this system, simply declared in 1661 that he would govern by himself rather than appoint a new first minister of state. It was a statement on his own identity as an absolute leader as much as it reflected his rights as king.

Absolutism emerged within the context of the religious and political conflicts that characterized the late Renaissance. Nearly every country with a Protestant population had engaged in religious warfare. This culminated in the Thirty Years' War (1618–1648), a series of interconnected wars across Europe built on religious alliances. Louis XIV's specific reforms sought to resolve the factionalism that characterized French politics during the 16th and 17th centuries. The French Wars of Religion (1562–1598) reflected deep divides over political priorities and religious reform, which became rooted in the monarch's own religious identity.

Louis XIV was motivated to make reforms by two political crises during his early reign. The first was the Fronde, a series of uprisings by various factions in France between 1648 and 1652 that were aimed at controlling the monarchy by replacing Louis' mother Anne and her advisors with nobles from another faction. This included Louis' cousin the Prince of Condé, who rebelled against the king and appealed for Spanish aid against the throne. The second was the English Civil War (1642–1651) between King Charles I and members of Parliaments, which was fought over English religious identity and disagreements over the role of Parliament in royal government. Louis's uncle, Charles I, was executed in 1649 at the height of the Fronde.

These events committed Louis XIV to eliminate rivalries over the nature of royal government. Ultimately he wanted an alternative to warfare to align his nobles with royal priorities. Jay Smith (1996) argues that royal authority became entrenched among the nobility because the French monarchy, beginning with Louis XIV, created a culture of merit in royal appointments. Absolutism opened government service to non-nobles and allowed a mechanism for social advancement that was much greater than could be achieved with an education during the Renaissance. This created a culture where power and authority were tied to the king's recognition of service. Elevation to nobility was the highest reward that a person could receive for good and faithful service.

To achieve these goals Louis XIV adapted parts of humanist culture to his new ideology. Versailles became an instrument of government and culture, where he required that courtesans be an *honnête homme*, a "man of honor, culture and erudition, self-controlled and well-mannered" (Wilkinson, 2018, p. 95). Louis took it upon himself to become the model for these character traits. He also relied on the classics to reinforce his public image; a task made possible because humanism had already become part of an aristocratic education. However, Louis relied far more on Greek mythology and literature than classical philosophy. Louis' favorite mythological figure was the sun-god Apollo, who symbolized the way the king's accomplishments shined forth on the French. In return, the glory and strength of the French people reflected the king's radiance.

Versailles represented the king's investment in his people and their reciprocal obligation to reinforce his authority. Louis XIV created a variety of academies to provide professional training in the arts and sciences. The goal was to create master craftsmen who could surpass the greatest artisans in the world. Versailles showcased their work. The Hall of Mirrors represented the finest products made in French factories. Its paintings symbolized the skill of French artists. The goal was to demonstrate that the French people had achieved an excellence beyond that of foreign competitors under the guidance of royal authority.

Louis XIV rearranged existing political relationships in a centralized system. He and his successors brought local governments into compliance by reforming the royal office of intendent, which was responsible for ensuring the collection of royal taxes. Leaders who cooperated with intendents received the king's endorsement in the form of royal permission to fulfill their role. Those who resisted could send a representative to Versailles to complain, which brought them into the center of cultural re-education and the presence of the king. Studies by William Beik (1985), Hilton Root (1987), and Donna Bohanan (2001) show that Louis XIV leveraged local and regional rivalries to bring communities into compliance. The king wanted to make Versailles the primary location of conflict resolution so that he could transform royal justice into royal favor. This validated local institutions but reframed their privileges as deriving from the royal will.

The strategies used by Louis XIV to reinforce his authority and shape the direction of his country directly impacted the rest of Europe. His effectiveness as a military commander during the first 30 years of his reign augmented French borders and brought foreign dignitaries to Versailles to negotiate terms for peace. France became Europe's cultural center and a model of effective government. Augustus II, elector of Saxony, was so impressed when he visited the palace in 1687 that he dedicated his resources to build Zwinger palace in Dresden as a center of absolutist culture. Others tried to replicate the French system more completely, particularly Spain, which was governed by Louis XIV's grandson Philip V after the War of Spanish Succession (1701–1714). Most rulers simply adapted elements of French absolutism to fit within their existing structures.

Enlightenment's Response to Absolutism

Historians view the Enlightenment as a response to the culture of absolutism. Philosophes accepted the relationship between social cohesion and government. However, they viewed absolutism as fundamentally flawed. It allowed monarchs to assert their will over their people rather than represent their community's interests. Philosophes were appalled at the persecutions committed in the name of unity, especially the effort to purge religious dissent.[5] Absolute government was hardly the only target of Enlightenment disdain, but its tendency to control and constrain culture did as much to facilitate social and religious tensions as it did to solve them through cultural uniformity. For example, Adam Smith's economic theories were directly opposed to the mercantilism favored by absolute monarchs. Laissez-faire economic policies, which Smith argued represented natural law, required governments to relinquish control of trade. Thus, philosophes understood that the broad changes necessary to improve human life required new political systems.

Intellectual challenges to absolutism were influenced by political developments in England, particularly the "Glorious Revolution" of 1688, a Parliamentary coup against King James II in favor of his daughter Mary and her husband William of Orange from the Netherlands. This is seen as a pivotal moment in the development of representative governments because William and Mary's succession was based on their agreement to publish a Bill of Rights guaranteeing Parliament's role in government. The bill also established certain legal rights for the people of England that put restrictions on the justice system. The revolution definitively rejected absolutism, which at the time was attracting followers across Europe.

The Glorious Revolution also brought with it a series of other changes that seemed to improve England's prosperity and peace. Steve Pincus (2011) argues that the Parliamentary leaders who led the coup viewed the revolution as an act of fundamental change. They looked at competing political organizations and their benefits, choosing the Netherlands as a better model of prosperity and growth than the absolutism of Louis XIV's court. James II had been moving England closer to the French model. The revolutionaries were committed to a whole system of reorganization. As Pincus states, "the creation of the Bank of England, war against France, and religious toleration were all explicit goals of many of the revolutionaries" (p. 8). They thought that a government with broader political participation would produce a stronger state than one under a system of absolutism.

John Locke's *Two Treatises of Government* (1689/1988), published to justify the new reforms, became the starting point for Enlightenment debates on the relationship between government and society. Locke argued that political systems derived from natural human relationships rather than God's ordination. People came together for survival, and when groups became large enough, they entered a mutual compact for food, justice, and defense. The way a community naturally organized itself defined political leadership. Government reflected a social contract between a community's people and the leaders they placed in authority. Communities had the natural authority to change governments when their leaders no longer fulfilled the social contract.

French translations of Locke's second treatise began circulating in France in the early 18th century. His ideas resonated because England's transformation stood out compared to the rest of Europe's political systems. Baron of Montesquieu was inspired to write *The Spirit of the Laws* (1748/1989) after spending several years in England at the end of a long tour of Europe. He published the book anonymously at the conclusion of the War of Austrian Succession (1740–1748). His primary goal was to evaluate the relationship between laws, government, personal freedoms, and political liberty. Montesquieu presented the English government as the best possible model to guarantee political liberty, the idea that laws should protect people from harm but also allow them to do as much as possible without restrictions. He did not believe people could simply copy the English system. Laws and governments varied according to population, culture, history, and climate.

However, he did believe a government that combined the strengths of monarchy, aristocracy, and democracy could check their inherent weaknesses and ensure better legislation and a more careful process of reform.

The Spirit of the Laws would greatly influence the development of the United States' government after the American Revolution. Thomas Jefferson and some of the other founders were part of the Enlightenment and sought to adapt prevailing ideas to their new country.[6] Yet Montesquieu was not seeking an armed rebellion. He sought a better way to reshape society through legal reform, justifying the role of monarchy within a new system that could maintain order and make society more stable. The book took almost 20 years to complete, but the timing of its publication at the conclusion of a war between absolute monarchs sets its ideas against the larger goals of absolutism.

Montesquieu's ideas were challenged by the Genevan Jean-Jacques Rousseau, who represents the Enlightenment's influence on the non-elite. He thought that the philosophes of Paris were too immersed in an elite system of luxury to fully reform the system. Rousseau's *The Social Contract* (1762/2009) offered a fundamentally different approach to the nature of government based on a different theory of natural law. Building off earlier works, Rousseau argued that the social contract represented an agreement between the collective members of a community rather than a community and its government. By this reasoning, he viewed laws as a reflection of the people's General Will. He proposed that a Republic would be the best form of government since it is the only political organization that involves the community directly. This would guarantee that no single individual could impose their will on another.

Unlike his predecessors, Rousseau provided a justification to get rid of monarchy altogether. This rested on an idea of equality between citizens, and that good government represented a government of equals. It also relied on the development of civic virtue. He understood that some people would not have the interest, capacity, or sense of public ethics to govern according to the General Will. They would need to cede authority to those who could handle the responsibility of governing on behalf of the people. These ideas became particularly popular among those in the American colonies and France who became disaffected with their kings in the last quarter of the 18th century. However, few countries would fully embrace the political ideals of the Enlightenment until the 19th and 20th centuries. These publications did create greater pressure for European governments to respond to public pressure for reform.

Influence of Enlightenment Ideals

The Enlightenment gained its significance through the exchange of ideas. It reached farther than the Renaissance, as the intellectual discourse among the 18th-century elite filtered more broadly to the rest of society. At the same time, this was built from a long trajectory of social advancement that evolved from humanism. At its core, the Enlightenment was the work of a self-defined community, a Republic of Letters, bound together over long distances through printed texts and personal letters. Paris became the central hub for this communication because of its proximity to Versailles.

Dena Goodman (1996) defines the Republic of Letters as an international organization where learned individuals could engage each other on equal terms. She argues that "the Republic of Letters has the same status as the monarchy: in the 18th century, it too had a political culture constructed out of discursive practices and institutions" (p. 1). Philosophes came from a variety of backgrounds and lived throughout Europe and its colonies. All members held to the common purpose of using human reason to create a better society, one that could transform people across religious and political boundaries.

Political ideas and cultural criticism spread easily because absolutism shaped all aspects of society across Europe. It was a commonality that did not exist during the Renaissance. The Republic of Letters built its strength off the public institutions that Louis XIV had used to convey the principles of absolutism beyond aristocratic circles. Nearly all countries had academies of the arts, sponsored by their governments, that held annual competitions open to the public. These offered a visual representation of aristocratic culture. Tim Blanning (2002) comments that "by the middle of the eighteenth century, 'the public' had become established as not just *a* legitimate voice in aesthetic appreciation but as *the* most authoritative" (p. 107). Monarchies intended public culture to bring the bourgeois into their respective absolutist system. Instead, it became a battleground of ideas. This can be seen in the proliferation of coffeehouses. They were first established in 17th-century London as a place of equality among educated men to read and discuss newspapers. By the 18th century, they were a place for nobles and gentlemen to converse about politics, economics, and social issues.

Royal efforts at censorship inadvertently helped spread Enlightenment ideals. Salons became an alternative to the court culture at Versailles and other royal palaces across Europe. These were typically hosted by wealthy women, who invited men of letters to engage with other wealthy individuals in an exchange of ideas. They were a place to share restricted books, many of them published by free presses in the Netherlands or Swiss Confederation. Printing houses also produced an array of subscription publications that could be delivered to private residences across Europe. Diderot's *Encyclopédie* was the most important of these, as it allowed philosophes to publish work on a variety of topics for public consumption. These extended the reach of Enlightenment ideals into what became known as the 'public sphere.'

Public discourse about politics did have an impact on royal governments. It prompted some rulers to modify how they approached public policies. The most prominent example is Frederick II of Prussia, who became a recognized member of Enlightenment culture. In 1736 he began a lifelong written correspondence with the French philosophe Voltaire, who became a frequent visitor to the Prussian court after 1740. Voltaire would depict Frederick II as a true enlightened monarch who captured the spirit of the age. This was based not only on his own participation in philosophic discourse but on domestic policies that mirrored the types of freedoms desired by the Republic of Letters.

The method of 'enlightened absolutism' promoted by Frederick II retained the royal bureaucracy at the heart of absolutism but used Enlightenment ideals to define his approach toward the people. Michael Spicer (1998) comments that the "administrative system was one that was highly centralized and subject to detailed day-to-day supervision and control by the king" (p. 24). The goal was to reign in the nobility by making government service a meritocracy, providing the same benefits of social mobility that existed in the French system. Yet Frederick's approach to public culture was far different than French absolutism. He embraced the ideals of equality and freedom sought after by the Republic of Letters. Frederick was praised for his religious tolerance and commitment to intellectual freedom. Unlike most of his peers, Frederick legalized the freedom of the press. He also used the Prussian Academy of Sciences to sponsor French intellectuals. Voltaire, Diderot, and Immanuel Kant were among the more prominent philosophes to receive memberships to the academy.

The political violence of the late 18th century prompted more vigorous debates over the nature of government within the public sphere. Frederick II wrote a treatise of political philosophy, the *Essay on the Forms of Government and the Duties of Sovereigns* in 1777, at the height of the American Revolution (Frederick II, 2021, pp. 195–207). Although Frederick remained a neutral observer of the war, he engaged the ideas that had influenced the American revolutionaries. Frederick II argued that a monarch received his right to rule through a social contract rather than by divine right, but refuted Locke's idea that government could be changed if a king violated this agreement. This rejected the fundamental premise of the American Revolution. However, the treatise publicly opposed the political theory at the center of absolutism. Kings were servants of the state rather than its masters. He argued that a monarch held a preeminent position over a society of equals. The primary job of a king was to care for the people. This was done by preserving the law, which applied equally to all citizens regardless of rank or profession.

Frederick II's treatise reflects the way that the Enlightenment was changing the way royal governments engaged with their populations. Even Louis

XVI, the last absolute king of France, tried to shift his approach to the public by releasing an annual report on royal finances. This was a double-edged sword, as it opened government expenditure to public debate, even though he intended it to reassure the public that royal finances were secure. The biggest challenge to absolutism came from those with the knowledge and expertise to provide rival leadership. Revolutionary politics was one method to bring about political change. The American and French Revolutions typically mark the end of the Enlightenment, in part, because France was unable to replicate the success of the United States.

Industrial Revolution

The Industrial Revolution is often closely associated with the Enlightenment because it represents notions of progress as applied to economic and technological change. By the late 19th century, the concept was used as a historiographical framework to describe a period of transition in English history between ca. 1760 and 1840, highlighting the relationship between ideas and economic and social change. Because of space, the discussion here will be limited to the industrialization of the cloth industry and its influence in England. This would have a profound impact on the development of manufacturing in the United States and the rest of Europe by the 1840s. At that point, industrialization had entered a second phase, a revolution in transportation through the development of railroads. There has been no end to this process. Informational technology, particularly the internet, continues to reshape the relationship between economy and society.

The creation of machine factories to spin cotton into thread and then produce cloth resulted in the most rapid economic, social, and political changes in recorded history. It crystalized the transition from an agricultural to commercial economy, shifted the labor force from small towns to cities, and established the middle class as the most influential social group in England. The Industrial Revolution also generated a more diverse, and divisive, evaluation of its impact than either the Renaissance or the Enlightenment. Economic historians point to the increasing wealth and standards of living that allowed England to become a model for other countries. Social historians note that these benefits came with a cost to laborers and their families. Unregulated growth contributed to poverty and health problems in industrial cities. Industrialization also facilitated political reform and strengthened government oversight over private enterprises.

Industrialization was significant because it intersected with ongoing socio-economic and political changes. It developed alongside the Enlightenment and benefited from England's trade system. It reached every demographic, allowing trends that began in the Renaissance and Enlightenment to reach most of England's population. The following discussion can only offer a brief introduction to the development of this system and its influence. It focuses on the creation of the factory system, its socio-economic impact, and its implications on organizational leadership.[7]

Foundations for Industrial Change

The industrial revolution represents a convergence of factors that contributed to the development of the factory system. The enclosure movement of the early 18th century closed off public land for private farming and led to a large pool of unemployed laborers. Cheap labor was the necessary condition to make the factory system sustainable. It allowed capitalists a workforce that could make industrialization profitable. Enclosure also placed limitations on royal and aristocratic control over economic life. This enabled the creation of private economic property and a freer use of personal resources for the emerging Middle Class. Investments in technology rewarded entrepreneurialism. Entrepreneurs formed new businesses, which allowed for their own social mobility, and led to greater wealth for local communities and the English government.

These factors provided the conditions for industrial change, but the factory system itself represents an amalgamation of technology invented by people trying to improve their lives or solve complex problems in engineering. Joel Mokyr (2012) refers to this as the "Industrial Enlightenment," the application of scientific discovery and experimentation to the study of technology. The engineers and craftsmen who engaged in this process were influenced by Enlightenment ideals. They sought to achieve progress through the practical application of knowledge. That it was based on individuals seeking ways to enhance their own livelihoods is without question. Technologies that allowed for industrialization were created by people looking to make their own professions easier. They represented a separate demographic from those engaging in philosophical debates about culture and politics.

The development of industrial cloth manufacturing is the classic model. This relied on technological developments in cloth production, steam power, and iron production to create the industrial factory. These technologies were created in a competitive environment that others could witness when put into use. Charles More (2002) uses the concept 'knowledge capital' to explain this process. The more people who used a particular technology, the more likely it was for someone to learn from it and spin off new equipment in other industries. The factory system represents the culmination of more than 60 years of technological development through small innovations that influenced larger inventions. Industrialization was created through a series of individual circumstances that progressively influenced each other.

This process can be seen in the development of Richard Arkwright's factory system. Arkwright built his first cotton mill at Cromford in Derbyshire in 1771 after developing and patenting the Water Frame two years before. He was inspired after visiting several cotton mills. He hired the clockmaker John Kay to help him develop a machine that could produce yarn more efficiently. The Water Frame improved upon two earlier inventions, the flyer-and-bobbin and the roller-spinning machine. Arkwright was also aware of a newer technology patented by James Hargreaves in 1764 that was more efficient than the traditional spinning wheel. The Spinning Jenny allowed a single cotton spinner within the existing cottage industry to operate multiple spindles without feeding each line by hand. Arkwright developed the Water Frame to improve upon the output of the Spinning Jenny by combining previous technology in a new way. He adapted the type of rollers used in metal production instead of the traditional wheel design. He created a machine that could be attached to dozens of spindles, though it required a non-human power source, exponentially increasing his output.

The modern industrial factory grew out of this initial design as Arkwright continued to adapt other people's technology to improve his system. He patented a new carding machine in 1775 that included a feeder that had been invented by John Lees in 1772.[8] A few years later Samuel Crompton merged the technology used in the Spinning Jenny and the Water Frame to create the Spinning Mule. This provided the advantages of both machines by creating thread that was more uniform and stronger than either technology could produce on their own. Arkwright would combine these machines with a steam engine at Shudehill Mill in Manchester in 1783. This became a model for industrial expansion over the next 50 years, as steam-powered mechanized factories moved beyond cloth production to other industries.

Socio-economic Impact of Industrialization

Arkwright did not set out to fundamentally alter socio-economic relationships. He began his career as a self-employed craftsman who managed to adapt technology for his own personal benefit.[9] The earliest factories began as small businesses operated directly by their owners. Yet Arkwright's system evolved to employ hundreds of people and run 24 hours a day, significantly changing the manufacturing industry. Factory owners were unable to monitor attendance and productivity on their own, leading to the development of new supervisor positions over the workforce. There were two basic approaches to organizing management. The earliest model was to employ master-craftsmen to hire, train, supervise, and fire workers on behalf of the owner. This offered an opportunity for skilled craftsmen to transfer their skills to a factory while maintaining a position of leadership over less-skilled workers. Over time the more common approach was to hire foremen from a factory's existing workforce. This offered opportunities for advancement to unskilled and semi-skilled workers based on merit and loyalty.

These practices had a polarizing impact on local communities. They did generate a type of social mobility for those fortunate to benefit from this new system. It established a new demographic who could share in the elite culture shaped by the Enlightenment. The entrepreneurs responsible for developing industrial technology were the first to experience socio-economic advantages. Not everyone who invented new technology gained wealth, but those who did managed to elevate their social standing. Richard Arkwright went from a poor wigmaker to a landed gentleman. He was able to use his early profits to finance factories in Manchester and other cities in northern England and Scotland. He received a knighthood in 1786 from King George III for his economic accomplishments and was made High Marshall of Derbyshire the following year. This success shaped his family for generations. His only surviving son inherited the family business, establishing his own career as an economic leader.

Factories had various effects on laborers and their families. They provided steady employment to the increasing number of rural poor impacted by the agricultural changes of the early 18th century. Emma Griffin (2013) observes that workers who left behind memoirs generally remarked that "work in cottage industry, factories, mines, warehouses, large cities and construction was better than the labour that had consumed their father's energies – and often their own early labours as well" (p. 46). Agricultural work tended to be seasonal and generally paid less than factories. This impacted the rural economy. Craftsmen often struggled to make a living, and in turn, offered fewer opportunities for apprenticeships. The best option for many was to find work in one of the growing manufacturing cities.

This benefited unskilled workers more than skilled craftsmen, who resented the development of technology that gave their competitors an advantage in cloth production. Skilled craftsmen could not maintain their income using traditional technology to produce yarn or cloth. They faced unemployment and poverty unless they transferred their skills to a factory. Factory work not only meant the loss of autonomy and control that most of them had enjoyed since the Middle Ages, but it brought a loss in status and income as they were compelled to do tasks that were suitable for unskilled labor.

Resistance to industrial technology was one outcome from these changes. This tended to come from skilled craftsmen rather than rural workers. This process began well before the industrial factory was in place. For example, James Hargreaves and others who used the Spinning Jenny faced opposition from those who couldn't afford the machine. Yet factories tended to face more organized resistance. The most volatile resistance took place during the 1810s by a coalition of weavers, croppers, and hosiers who could no longer compete against the machines used in cloth factories. The Luddite movement was a series of frame-breaking protests that began in Nottingham and spread to Lancashire and Yorkshire between 1811 and 1816.

The Luddites were inspired by an earlier frame-breaking movement in 1779 that was supposedly led by a young apprentice named Ned Ludd. E. J. Hobsbawn (1952) characterizes the Luddites as an early form of organized labor. He regards their practice of frame-breaking as a type of "collective bargaining by riot" (p. 59). Luddites would send letters in the name of "General Ludd" to factory owners and city leaders prior to breaking into local factories. They demanded that new machines be removed, and skilled labor be hired instead, or they would wreck the machines. Luddites destroyed thousands of frames throughout the midlands and northern England to prevent unemployment and maintain their standard of living.

The Luddite revolts reflect many problems associated with the industrialization of England. Perhaps the most important was the inability for local leaders to manage the social impact of rapid economic change. The British government's response, influenced by their fear that frame breaking would lead to political violence, extended this problem into national politics. Parliament passed the Frame Breaking Act in February 1812, which provided the death penalty for anyone who broke into a factory or damaged a frame. The government also authorized the use of British troops to defend factories and prevent riots.

The government's response suppressed Luddism but transformed the popular movement into an organized effort to create political change. This extended the political debates of the Enlightenment more firmly into the realm of labor. Local governments reacted harshly to collective activism, the Peterloo Massacre being the most dramatic and highly publicized. On August 16, 1819, civic leaders in Manchester ordered the British cavalry to disperse approximately 60,000 people who had gathered to listen to members of the Manchester Patriotic Union advocate for the expansion of voting rights. Eleven people were killed and more than 600 were injured, including women and children. The incident would prompt greater attention into problems associated with industrialization.

Broader Significance of Industrial Change

Industrialization transplanted people into a new environment and recreated local communities. This did not create the type of integrated society that humanists or philosophes used as the basis for their organizational theories. Some factory owners did invest in housing and select service industries to help support their workers. This transformed cotton mills into factory towns that could mitigate the impact of mass migration on surrounding areas.[10] However, factory towns were based on the production of goods rather than the creation of a community. Most factory owners did not seek to create relational bonds with their workforce, as leaders during the Renaissance tried to do through the sponsorship of humanism. They were more interested in establishing social and economic ties with other members of the elite.

The development of organized labor and political reform were two of the most important outcomes from this environment. These developed gradually as efforts to bring productive change locally failed to reach acceptable solutions. A few factory owners attempted to transform management to better integrate workers into their organizations. For example, Robert Owen worked on an alternative model of factory management after observing the harsh treatment often used to increase productivity. Tim Hatcher (2013) views these efforts as an early example of human resource development. Owen viewed his duty as a manager to create an acceptable work environment and care for his employees. He banned corporal punishment and built a system that relied on trust and positive reinforcement to motivate his workforce.[11]

Few owners were interested in creating the type of community required by Owen's system. Part of this was due to rapidly changing demographics that worked against the concept of factory towns in England by the early 1800s. The steam engine allowed owners to concentrate factories in the same area, leading to the development of industrial cities. The city of Manchester became the center of the cotton industry. There were 86 cotton mills operating along or near the Bridgewater Canal by 1816. Working-class neighborhoods merged into the old town without any systematic planning. As a result, the city had insufficient housing, inadequate sewage, and poor water supply.[12]

These problems would change the way civic leaders managed their cities and redefined their relationship with the national government. For example, Manchester's traditional organizational structure lacked the political authority or resources to manage rapid urban development. The city's inhabitants were responsible for organizing ways to promote health and safety themselves. They could only address symptoms of industrial change. Some of city's elite established the Poor Committee in 1793 to better distribute poor relief. They created the first soup kitchen in 1799, which became a permanent charity the following decade. Thomas Percival helped establish the Manchester Board of Health in 1795, a voluntary organization aimed at improving sanitation. He and fellow board members investigated factories and lobbied Parliament to improve working conditions. This influenced Robert Peel's Health and Morals of Apprentices Act of 1802, the first bill to regulate factories.

Others worked towards enabling laborers to participate more fully in public life. Religious outreach programs allowed workers to develop their own means to address socio-economic problems. The Methodists were particularly successful in transforming laboring families. Their teachings on spiritual equality allowed workers to share in church ministry and gain leadership within community programs. Griffin (2013) comments that this outreach allowed the working class to gain independence from their social superiors in a church environment, inviting them to share their ideas in public. These programs "helped create a workforce with the capacity for collective action" (p. 189).

This enabled workers to develop Mutual Improvement Societies aimed at furthering their education and offering financial support in times of crisis. By the 1810s workers began developing their own political organizations, especially after the failure of the Luddite revolts. Midland and northern workers established Hampden clubs in 1816 as a venue for political debate. Suppression by local authorities the following year led to the development of the Patriotic Union Society. It was the Manchester branch of this organization that created the meeting at St. Peter's Field in August 1819 that led to the Peterloo Massacre.

The violence associated with the Luddites and the Peterloo Massacre intersected with larger political debates that originated in the 17th century. The Industrial Revolution was a catalyst to further political reform, facilitating the English government's transformation into a Parliamentary democracy. It added new voices to public political discourse, extending an important legacy from the Enlightenment to new groups of people. Parliament would respond to public pressure by passing a series of acts between 1832 and 1848 that would begin changing voting rights and guide the way local governments managed industrial growth. The Industrial Revolution was not *the* cause of political change in England, but it did lead many people to see Parliament as the only leadership body capable of providing wholistic reform.

Conclusion

The Renaissance, Enlightenment, and Industrial Revolution are important because of their immediate impact and ongoing influence. The focus here has been to introduce the basic elements of these movements and their cumulative effect. Humanists during the 15th and 16th centuries sought to generate better leadership by emulating qualities promoted by Roman statesmen. A classical education was only the beginning. Humanist leaders crafted organizational stability by investing in a common culture that bound their communities together. The Enlightenment developed out of humanism's inability to bring broader stability to Europe. Monarchies tried to impose a common value system to bring their people into alignment with royal priorities. Philosophes rearranged this relationship by placing leadership as an outgrowth of organizational culture. The Industrial Revolution developed alongside the Enlightenment, dramatically altering socio-economic relationships, which accelerated the influence of public discourse on political change.

This discussion provides only a partial picture of each movement. The aim has been to illustrate by example key features of a historical mindset, demonstrating how history accounts for continuity and change by situating long-term trends within the circumstances that contributed to their development, growth, and adaptation. Historical sensemaking recognizes that people are part of complex systems that have short- and long-term antecedents. People respond to immediate events based on their own cultural upbringing, previous experiences, relationship to other people, and external factors that intersect their lives. No single person or event created the Renaissance, Enlightenment, or Industrial Revolution. Those who helped shape these movements were as much a product of their times as they were innovators. Their significance relied on their ability to influence the people around them; their ideas and actions gained relevance because enough people were willing to accept them as alternatives to the status quo. This interaction forms new contexts that shape later settings.

History's value rests in its ability to explain the past and draw out its significance. This can only happen when both the past and the present are viewed historically, placing events and ideas in their respective contexts to isolate patterns that persist through time. History becomes useful when commonalities can be explained through their individual settings and then compared. For example, Industrial factories were built around a transactional relationship between owners and their workforce. While this concept was not new, industrialization had a ripple effect on nearly every community or institution without building a strong basis for relational stability. It lacked the common intellectual and cultural cohesiveness that were important during the Renaissance and Enlightenment. This is where the earlier models of leadership become relevant, with the understanding that they must be adapted to new environments.

The socio-economic challenges associated with the factory system demonstrate that the attributes associated with effective leadership in earlier eras matter as much in a business setting as they do in other organizations. This offers some parallels to the observations made by James MacGregor Burns (1978) on transformational leadership in the political arena. As will be seen in chapter three, the challenges brought by industrialization led to the development of organizational theories aimed at addressing efficiency and human capital. This research led to the discovery that thriving companies were more productive when perceived as shared human endeavors driven by common values. This emphasis on core values as the means for unity and stability applies equally in the 21st century as it did in the 15th century. History informs values and provides methods for adapting them to new circumstances. Chapters four and five elucidate on history's role in shaping effective leadership practices.

Notes

1. As an example, see Brotten's *The Renaissance Bazaar* (2002), which places the Renaissance in a global context rather than a specific Italian movement.
2. The Byzantine Empire represents the Greek speaking successors to the Roman Empire. By the 14th century their territory had been reduced to parts of modern-day Turkey and the Aegean. The Ottoman Turks appeared from the Eurasian Steppe in the 14th century, conquering the Greeks and extending their empire into Eastern Europe during the next three centuries.
3. John D'Amico's *Renaissance Humanism in Papal Rome* (1983) offers a comprehensive study on papal sponsorship of humanism before the Reformation.
4. Calvinism is named after John Calvin, representing his core theological ideas and organizational principles. As can be seen in a recent biography by Gordon (2009), Calvin's ideas were shaped by his interaction with religious and secular leaders on both sides of the confessional divide between Protestantism and Catholicism.
5. Louis XIV and his successors tried to reinforce cultural conformity with religious conformity. To be French was to be Catholic. To these ends the monarchy ended its tolerance of Protestants, which had been a condition of peace after the wars of religion in 1598. The monarchy also tried to purge a Catholic faction known as the Jansenists. They believed that God's will above the king's, thus diminishing royal authority over the French people.
6. American historiography has a long tradition of looking back at the Enlightenment as creating the ethos for the United States. Caroline Winterer's *American Enlightenment* (2016) is a recent addition to this tradition and offers a good overview of this historiographic tradition in its introduction.
7. For a more comprehensive discussion of of the Industrial Revolution see Allen (2009) and Hudson (2009).
8. A carding machine prepares raw cotton for spinning.
9. For more on Richard Arwright's life and influences, see Fitton (1989).
10. Richard Arkwright developed Cromford Mill as a factory town with a row of cottages for his workers less than one mile from his mill. He established a Saturday market and sponsored farms to provide fresh produce for his workers and their families, closing the mill on Sunday so that they could attend services in a church that he built onsite. This allowed workers to maintain Arkwright's strict work-schedule while giving them easy access to the amenities needed to support their families.
11. Day to day management was based on a "Silent Monitor" rating system. Each day supervisors would rate worker performance and leave a mark on each machine that could be seen by every worker. Those who consistently received high marks were rewarded. The goal was to motivate low achievers to model their performance off the best workers. Owen relied on his workforce to enforce this system, creating leaders among his workers to implement changes.
12. For more on the Industrial Revolution's impact on cities, see Vigier (1970), Williamson (2009), and Maw (2013).

References

Allen, R. C. (2009). *The British industrial revolution in global perspective*. Cambridge University Press.

Beik, W. (1985). *Absolutism and society in seventeenth-century France: State power and provincial aristocracy in Languedoc*. Cambridge University Press.

Blanning, T. (2002). *The culture of power and the power of culture*. Oxford University Pres.

Bohanan, D. (2001). *Crown and nobility in early modern France*. Palgrave.

Bouwsma, W. J. (1990). Calvinism as a renaissance artifact. In T. George (Ed.), *John Calvin and the Church: A prism of reform* (pp. 28–41). Westminster/John Knox Press.

Brotton, J. (2002). *The Renaissance Bazaar: From the Silk Road to Michelangelo*. Oxford University Press.

Brucker, G. A. (1957). The Medici in the fourteenth century. *The Speculum 32*(1), 1–26.

Burckhardt, J. (1860/1990). *The civilization of the renaissance in Italy*. Penguin Books.

Burns, J. M. (1978). *Leadership*. Harper Perennial.

Castiglione, B. (1528/1976). *The book of the courtier* (Rev. ed.). (G. Bull, Trans.). Penguin Classics.

D'Amico, J. F. (1983). *Renaissance Humanism in Papal Rome: Humanists and Churchmen on the Eve of Reformation*. The John Hopkins University Press.

Erasmus, D. (1989). *The praise of Folly and other writings* (R.M. Adams, Ed.). W.W. Norton & Company.

Fitton, R. S. (1989). *The arkwrights: Spinners of fortune*. Manchester University Press.

Frederick II. (2021). *Frederick the Great's Philosophical Writings* (A. Lifschitz, Ed.; A. Scholar, Trans.). Princeton University Press.

Goodman, D. (1996). *The republic of letters: A cultural history of the French enlightenment*. Cornell University Press.

Gordon, B. (2009). *Calvin*. Yale University Press.

Griffin, E. (2013). *Liberty's dawn: A people's history of the industrial revolution*. Yale University Press.

Hatcher, T. (2013). Robert Owen: A historiographical study of a pioneer of human resource development. *European Journal of Training and Development, 37*(4), 414–431.

Hobsbawn, E. J. (1952). The machine breakers. *Past and Present, 1*(1), 57–70.

Hudson, Pat. (2009). *The industrial revolution*. Bloomsbury.

Jurdjevic, Mark. (1999). Civic humanism and the rise of the medici. *Renaissance Quarterly, 52*(4), 994–1020.

Kent, D. (2000). *Cosimo De' Medici and the Florentine Renaissance: The Patron's Oeuvre*. Yale University Press.

Locke, J. (1689/1988). *Two treatises of government* (P. Laslett, Ed.). Cambridge University Press.

Machiavelli, N. (1532/1998). *The prince* (2nd ed., H.C. Mansfield, Trans.). University of Chicago Press.

Martines, L. (2003). *April blood: Florence and the plot against the medici*. Oxford University Press.

Maw, P. (2013). *Transport and the industrial city: Manchester and the canal age, 1750–1850*. Manchester University Press.

Maxon, B. J. (2014). *The humanist world of renaissance florence*. Cambridge University Press.

Mokyr, J. (2012). *The enlightened economy: An economic history of Britain 1700–1850*. Yale University Press.

Montesquieu. (1748/1989). *The spirit of the laws* (A. M. Cohler, B. C. Miller, H. S. Stone, Trans. and Eds.). Cambridge University Press.

More, C. (2002). *Understanding the industrial revolution*. Routledge.

Padgett, J. F., & Ansell, C. K. (1993). Robust action and the rise of the medici, 1400–1434. *The American Journal of Sociology*, 98(6), 1259–1319.

Pincus, S. (2011). *1688: The frist modern revolution*. Yale University Press.

Root, H. L. (1987). *Peasants and king in Burgundy: Agrarian foundations of French absolutism*. University of California Press.

Rousseau, J. J. (1762/2009). *The social contract* (C. Betts, Trans.). Oxford University Press.

Smith, J. M. (1996). *Nobility, Royal Service, and the Making of Absolute Monarchy in France, 1600–1789*. The University of Michigan Press.

Spicer, M. W. (1998). Public administration under "enlightened despotism" in Prussia: An examination of Frederick the great's administrative practice. *Administrative Theory & Praxis*, 20(1), 23–31.

Vigier, I. (1970). *Change and apathy: Liverpool and Manchester during the industrial revolution*. MIT Press.

Wilkinson, R. (2018). *Louis XIV* (2nd ed.). Routledge.

Williamson, J. G. (2009). *Coping with city growth during the British industrial revolution*. Cambridge University Press.

Winterer, C. (2016). *American Enlightenment: Pursuing Happiness in the Age of Reason*. Yale University Press.

3   A Brief History of Leadership and Organizational Studies

In the Beginning – Rational Systems

Formal organizations are everywhere and unavoidable. People are born, educated, governed, employed, married, and buried in formal organizations. It is difficult to imagine a society, government, business, school, and even a home existing without some level of formal or officially sanctioned structures. There is even an organization that helps organizations that exist exclusively to help leaders better govern their respective organizations, the American Society of Association Executives (ASAE).[1]

Since creation, people have preferred order over chaos, predictability over randomness, and rules over anarchy. People have created structures and systems since day one to become more efficient and effective in their collective endeavors. How and why people organize the way they do has changed over time, yet the need to organize has remained constant. Each period in the history of formal organizations was a corrective to the previous systems or a response to societal changes. The different periods of organizational history reveal different facets of the collective and provide leaders and managers with multiple frames of reference to optimize outcomes.

In the beginning, or at least in premodern societies, tribal villages had little need for formal organizations as people know them today. Families survived and thrived by working together, whether in nomadic or farming communities, each doing different jobs as necessary for the good of the whole. Individuals and families banded together out of affinity and loyalty to tribal members to cooperate for the good of the group. As families and communities expanded, new structures were needed. As technological advancements created new efficiencies, the nature of community changed.

The sociologist Ferdinand Tönnies (1855–1936) described the substantive differences between living in a community and in a society in his 1887 treatise, *Community and Civil Society*. Communities, in contrast to societies, are organic collectives where people are "bound together by ties of

DOI: 10.4324/9781003100171-3

kinship, fellowship, custom, history and communal ownership of primary goods" (Harris, 2001, pp. xvii–xviii). In communities, people cooperate out of natural affinity with its members. Tönnies noted:

> All kinds of social co-existence that are familiar, comfortable and exclusive are to be understood as belonging to *Gemeinschaft* [community]. . . . In *Gemeinschaft* we are united from the moment of our birth with our own folk for better or worse.
>
> (p. 18)

As local communities grew in size and complexity and began to overlap with other local communities, it became difficult to discern strangers from neighbors. New modes of cooperation were needed when kinship and natural affinity groups were no longer dominant or present. As the Industrial Revolution displaced people from family farms and local communities to industrial cities, people had to rely on the cooperation of strangers to co-exist.

Societies, in contrast to communities, are more mechanical collectives "where free-standing individuals interacted with each other through self-interest, commercial contracts, a 'spatial' rather than a 'historical' sense of mutual awareness, and the external constraints of formally enacted laws" (Harris, 2001, p. xviii). Tönnies (1887/2001) noted:

> The theory of *Gesellschaft* [society] takes as its starting point a group of people who, as in *Gemeinschaft*, live peacefully alongside one another, but in this case without being essentially united – indeed, on the contrary, they are here essentially detached. In *Gemeinschaft* they stay together in spite of everything that separates them; in *Gesellschaft* they remain separate in spite of everything that unites them.
>
> (p. 52)

Communities have a familial atmosphere, and cooperation is almost always unconditional because everyone is an insider. Societies have a contractual feel and cooperation is conditional because people feel like outsiders. This transition from *gemeinschaft* to *gesellschaft* happened when people relocated from "community by *blood*, indicating primal unity of existence" into "community of *place*, which is expressed first of all as living in close proximity to one another" (Tönnies, 1887/2001, p. 27). Communities of place became the norm because of the Industrial Revolution and ushered the need for organizations to develop more formal structures and policies to facilitate cooperation since communities of kinship had diminished. The first assembly line factories are a classic example. They used money to get desperate workers to coordinate their efforts and increase output. This contrasted life in the rural communities, where members of the community generally cooperated out of affinity toward one another.

The first period of the modern organization in civil society that formally systematized cooperation was the rational structural system approach advocated by Max Weber (1864–1920) and Frederick Taylor (1856–1915).[2] Weber, also a sociologist, introduced the rational bureaucracy with its clearly defined hierarchies, division of labor with specialized roles, and rules and regulations. The Weber bureaucracy created formal structures to coordinate cooperation and maximize efficiencies, becoming the standard blueprint for managing factories and companies (Weber, 1905; Weber, 1922).

Taylor, a mechanical engineer, applied the scientific method to Weber's bureaucracy to optimize efficiencies. Taylor conducted experiments to increase production with as few employees as necessary. He documented that maximum efficiency and productivity was ensured by proper selection, training, and supervision of employees along with streamlined production systems. Taylor's (1911) *The Principles of Scientific Management* reflected and shaped the zeitgeist of that period.

Schools adopted the factory model of efficiency, vestiges of which remain today with a bell schedule determining learning shifts, large schools with multiple classrooms off the main corridors to efficiently manage traffic flow, and a 'superintendent' of schools in charge of coordinating the school plant activities. Frank (1868–1924) and Lillian (1878–1972) Gilbreth, both distinguished engineers, conducted time motion studies ranging from brick laying, cooking in the home kitchen to surgical procedures in hospitals. They applied the principles from their famous studies of breaking tasks down to their simplest motions, to managing their household of 12, which became the basis for the book, *Cheaper by the Dozen* (Gilbreth & Careym, 1948), co-authored by two of their children.

Taylorism also transformed the nature of commerce in the United States. In 1925, during his tenure as Secretary of Commerce, Herbert Hoover stated in a speech before the United States Chamber of Commerce, "I believe that we are in the presence of a new era which the organization of industry and commerce in which, if properly directed, lie forces pregnant with infinite possibilities of more progress" (Odell, 1925, p. 327). That new era was bringing business into government to eliminate waste and promote the collective efficiencies of industry. Hoover served as secretary of commerce from 1921to 1928 and worked zealously to improve "living standards through the standardizations of living," using the principles of scientific management that have proved so useful in the business sector (Busch, 2017, p. 35).

Prior to Hoover's tenure as Secretary of Commerce, U.S. commerce was not as coordinated as it is known for today. While individual organizations were efficient, the organizational fields were inefficient and wasteful. For example, individual factories were efficient in making bedsteads, but the lack of standard sizes made the collective industry less efficient with the production of one custom-sized bedstead, requiring the subsequent production of a custom mattress and a shipping crate. Hoover realized that if there were standard measurements of bed frames, then mattresses and shipping boxes could be made equally standardized to increase the overall efficiency of the organizational field by eliminating waste and simplifying production. He changed the variety of beds from 78 to 4 sizes (Busch, 2017, p. 58). He did the same with milk bottles, changing the amount "from 49 to 9, while the number of caps was reduced from 29 to 1" (Busch, p. 58). During his tenure as Secretary of Commerce, "86 industries simplified practices resulting in a claimed $600 million savings to customers" (Busch, 2017, p. 57). Standardization of products, fittings (nut, bolts, and screws), and batteries make stores like Home Depot and Lowes possible and profitable and has simplified the work of do-it-yourself homeowners.

The rational scientific management approach legitimatized military precision for organizations and corresponding bureaucracies to efficiently manage large-scale operations. The emphasis on productivity axiomatically treated employees as cogs in the production line who were expected to perform their duties in a mechanical fashion. It was a later set of efficiency experiments that led to the accidental, yet inevitable, discovery of the power of social attitudes in the workplace and the inadequacies of the rational structural approach to understand fully the nature and work of the collective. While people were living and working in communities of place, they were by nature creating communities of affinity, *pseudo-blood* communities.

Natural Systems

As social scientists continued to conduct efficiency studies, an industrial psychologist by the name of Elton Mayo (1880–1949) and his team made an accidental discovery of why and how people ultimately perform the way they do in the workplace. Mayo was investigating the relationship between work conditions and employee productivity in the Hawthorne Works of the Western Electric Company located on the West Side of Chicago. When the study commenced in 1927, the company "employed approximately 29,000 workers, representing some 60 nationalities" (Roethlisberger & Dickson, 1939/1961, p. 6). A series of studies on different work conditions, including how much illumination the factory floor needed, was conducted to optimize efficiencies and output. The initial results revealed that something else besides physical work conditions was influencing output, resulting in additional studies at the Hawthorne site for the next five years. Mayo and his team discovered that varying the conditions on the work floor, such as lighting, did not impact output as expected, but rather the fact that the workers on the floor knew that they were being observed by social scientists heightened their levels of engagement. The Hawthorne studies discovered that worker output was better explained by informal rules and social norms inherent in various subgroups than by formal rules and expectations.[3]

The conclusions of the study enlarged the view of organizations as having two major functions. In their detailed account of the Hawthorne Study, researchers on Mayo's team, Roethlisberger and Dickson (1939/1961) noted:

> The first function is ordinarily called economic. From this point of view the function of the concern is assessed in such terms as cost, profit, and technical efficiency. The second function, while it is readily understood, is not ordinarily designated by any generally accepted word. It is variously described as maintaining employee relations, employee good will, co-operation, etc. From this standpoint the function of concern is frequently assessed in such terms as labor turnover, tenure of employment, sickness and accident rate, wages, employee attitudes, etc. The industrial concern is continually confronted, therefore with two sets of major problems: (1) problems of external balance, and (2) problems of internal equilibrium.
>
> (p. 552)

The "logic of sentiments" – people's beliefs and values among different working groups within the organization are equally, if not more, important as the "logic of efficiency." All organizations consist of formal and informal rules and "the limits of human collaboration are determined more by the informal than by the formal organization of the plant" (Roethlisberger & Dickson, 1939/1961, p. 568). While what employees think, feel, and value in their work naturally matters, it was a relatively new epiphany in 1932.

The Hawthorne studies documented that people have an affinity for community, that intangible factors affected employee engagement, and that organizations are social systems with stated (rational model) and unstated rules; ideas advocated by Mary Parker Follett (1868–1933) a few decades earlier. Peter Drucker (1995) called Follet the "prophet of management" (p. 9). She challenged the precepts of scientific management and introduced human psychology in organizational administration, and influenced the work of Chester Barnard, Peter Drucker, Kurt Lewin, and Abraham Maslow. She argued that relationships matter more than transactions in organizations and determined the level of engagement and cooperation, replaced the notion of "power over" with "power with" to reflect the reality and synergy of collaboration, posited that conflict was constructive and necessary for wisdom, highlighted how the common purpose is the invisible and critical leader of any group, and tasked leaders to train followers to be leaders in the workplace (Metcalf & Urwick, 1942; Follet, 1924).

Another luminary in the human relations movement was Chester Barnard (1886–1961). He was the Executive President of New Jersey Bell Telephone, served as president of the USO (United Services Organization, Inc.) during World War II, and ended his career as the president of the Rockefeller Foundation. He published two seminal books, *The Functions of the Executive* (1938) and *Organization and Management* (1948), that established the importance of formal and informal cooperation in organizations. Barnard demonstrated that while executives may impose goals from the top down, the conditions of a community determine how and when such goals are fulfilled from the bottom up. Barnard used the concept of "zones of indifference" to capture the nature of individual and collective psycho-social contracts in the workplace and when compliance and cooperation happened between managers and employees:

> The zone of indifference will be wider or narrower depending upon the degree which the inducements exceed the burdens and sacrifices which determine the individual's adhesion to the organization. It follows that the range of orders that will be accepted will be very limited among those who are barely induced to contribute to the system.
>
> (Barnard, 1938, p. 169)

Properly induced employees are happy, loyal, and engaged employees. Managers only have authority to the extent employees willingly confer it upon them. Not only did Barnard challenge the traditional notions of cooperation and authority, but he also brought to the forefront the roles of common purpose and motivation in the workplace. McNally (2018) noted that Barnard's effort "to link organizational success and failure with human needs and attitudes was a 'landmark in management thought that stands to this day' (Wren, 1994, p. 267)" (p. 112).

The human relations system revealed the need and advantages to expand the role of human resource personnel and offices from compliance to include a more holistic approach of employee development and engagement. It led to the creation of professional organizations like the Society for Human Resource Management (SHRM), the National Human Resources Association (NHRA), and the International Public Management Association for Human Resources (IPMA-HR), again documenting the propensity toward organizing organizations. The now commonplace practice for organizations to offer competitive employee benefits and reward plans with vacation and sick days to recruit and retain top talent has its roots in human relations research.

The logics of efficiency and sentiment captured how and why organizations perform as they do. They also reveal that managers and leaders must attend to both the formal and informal structures and human needs and wants. As organizations and organizational fields expanded and became more complex, other governing logics emerged. There was a transition from operating organizations solely in closed systems to recognizing that larger environmental considerations influenced organizational performance.

Open and Complex Adaptive Systems

The railroad industry transformed society by allowing people and organizations to efficiently connect with one another. Advantageous interdependencies within and across organizations were created due to the convenience and speed by which people could communicate, and products and services could be exchanged over the rail. The telephone, automobile, airplane, and computer were game changers for similar reasons. These formal and informal connections gave way to necessary networks and created temperamental organizational ecosystems. The 1918 Spanish flu and recent COVID pandemics that temporarily shut the world down are two examples, albeit extreme, of how people and organizations are interconnected and vulnerable to larger environmental conditions.

While the railroad industry primarily resides in a relatively linear and closed system bound by rail tracks and time schedules, its efficiencies are nonetheless impacted by external factors such as weather, natural disasters, employee morale and relations, safety and security considerations, and routine and unexpected maintenance. In contrast, the maritime commerce industry resides primarily in a dynamic open system and is much more at the mercy of fate,[4] at least in the 17th century, and made evident by a careful reading of Moby Dick.

It was in the maritime global economy of the 17th century that the Lloyd's of London was founded. Originally a coffee house on Tower Street, Lloyd's was a place in the 1680s where ship captains and owners and moneymen gathered to negotiate contracts to insure shipping ventures against probable loss. Lloyd's coffee house, founded in 1687, started to attract more selective patrons and established a reputation as the go-to place for reliable marine insurance (Flower & Jones, 1974). Edward Lloyd, the proprietor gave the insurance market a place to conduct business and eventually a formal "doing business as" name for the esteemed group of underwriters (Gibb, 1924).[5] Eventually, the underwriters relocated and formed their own trust, marking the start of Lloyds of London proper. The Lloyd's Act of 1871 incorporated the "members of the Establishment or Society formerly held at Lloyd's Coffee House in the Royal Exchange in the City of London" (The Corporation of Lloyd's, 1871). Three hundred thirty-one years later, Lloyd's of London remains the world's specialist insurance marketplace, an industry that gives evidence businesses are vulnerable to unknown and unanticipated risks and are at the mercy of fate.

Industrial enterprises mushroomed during the Industrial Revolution creating greater interdependences and concentrations of risk. Correspondingly, overcrowded cities became the norm, which ushered attendant risks associated with unsanitary and unsafe living conditions. The devastating Bubonic Plague of London (1665–1666), Great Fire of London (1666), and Great Chicago Fire (1871) were disasters waiting to happen because of the inherent risks associated with contemporary cities at the time. The Enlightenment made possible a new and profitable industry devoted to financial recovery from unwelcomed and unplanned losses for the common person and small business owners, an equivalent of a Lloyd's but at a smaller scale.

The modern insurance industry emerged as a "counterbalance to the new and potentially destabilizing forces that were transforming the division of labour, urbanisation, and the economics of trade" (Haueter, 2017, p. 9). Prior to the Enlightenment and subsequent social and economic changes associated with the Industrial Revolution, extended families came to the rescue when members of the community suffered loss from natural disasters, debilitating accidents, prolonged illness, and death of loved ones. New systems and structures were needed in a civil society (*gesellschaft*) to alleviate financial loss when community (*gemeinschaft*) was no longer available or sufficient to weather hardship when fate was particularly unkind. Haueter (2017) documented that:

> The Age of Reason or Enlightenment of the 17th and 18th centuries provided the grounds for accepting actuarial science as a rational means to conduct better business. Insurance, and especially life insurance, resonated with the search for laws, the statistical recording of natural events and the calculation of future developments. Behind this innovation was the conviction that the world, and its possible future states, could be predicted and computed.
>
> (p. 9)

The modern-day insurance industry is testimony that while events and patterns of events are relatively predictable, risks always lurk in the environment, especially when systems reach a point of self-organized criticality when one disruption can have a cascading effect (e.g., perfect storm events). Organizational leaders and managers have always attempted to mitigate the risks associated with uncertainty, whether by primarily appealing to God's providence before the Renaissance, securing insurance since the Enlightenment, and engaging in strategic planning since the Late Modern Period.

As the world became more interconnected and advances in technology allowed for faster collaboration and calculations, physical and social scientists working in a variety of fields simultaneously discovered similar levels of complexity in their respective systems. The additional competing logics associated with the emergence of growing and expanding networks and collective efficiencies exposed nonlinear and nonrational elements in organizational activities. Institutional theory and complexity science yielded new insights to anticipating and managing organizational risk and uncertainty, not accounted for in the rational and natural systems frameworks and not necessarily covered by prayer or insurance.

Barabási and Bonabeau (2003) stated that scientists have "discovered that various complex adaptive systems have an underlying architecture governed by shared organizing principles" (p. 50). Shoup and Studer (2010) identified seven features common to all complex adaptive systems (CAS) and documented how leaders and managers need to take a systemic approach to optimize the performance of their respective collectives. The short version is that organizations are embedded in the larger economic, political, social, and physical environments and that "business as usual" involves balancing multiple and competing expectations and demands with limited resources. As a result, thriving organizations continuously adapt and make mid-course corrections. Leaders and managers not only need to be as efficient as possible (rational systems) and attend to the psycho-social wellbeing of their stakeholders (natural systems), but they must also anticipate and manage change to maintain stability and survive (open systems).

Complexity science also explains why history at the macro and micro levels tends to repeat itself, albeit on different scales.

> While history is chronological, a strictly linear presentation reinforces the false reductionist paradigm that the events of today and tomorrow are the result of yesterday's events. Complexity reveals history as another version of the present and future. A long-term perspective on history reveals patterns are at work in the universe. History cannot but help repeat itself, not because people are forgetful or ignorant of the past, but because the dominant values at work in the past are at work in both the present and future.
>
> (Shoup & Studer, p. 24)

From this framework, history and organizational practices are best viewed as a swinging pendulum, each oscillation of change keeps the overall system in relative equilibrium. The pendulums' pattern is ultimately determined by the system's dominant values. Hence, the wisdom of the French proverb, *the more things change, the more they stay the same* and the aphorism that *what is past is prologue.*

The swinging pendulum in human affairs is nothing new. King Solomon noted in his brief memoir that "what has been, it is what will be, and what has been done, it is what will be done. So there is nothing new under the sun" (Ecclesiastes, 1:9). Theories of historical and cosmic cycles are found in the Vedas and Ancient Chinese and Greek writings and were recently documented by contemporary historians and social commentators. Williams and Drew (2012), in their book, *Pendulum*, demonstrated that social movements reappear approximately every 40 years and that "the 'dominant' twenty-year periods mark the upswing of a pendulum and the 'recessive' twenty-year periods mark its downswing, as the values that pushed the pendulum upward begin to run out of steam" (p. 9). Balkin (2020), in his book, *The Cycles of Constitutional Time*, developed the idea that "American political history has featured a series of successive governing regimes in which political parties compete" (p. 13) and documented the cycles of success and demise of Republican and Democratic regimes. The renowned historians Arthur Schlesinger, Sr. (1949) and Arthur Schlesinger, Jr. (1999), described patterns in government that oscillate between liberal and conservative movements in their books, *Paths to the Present* and *The Cycles of American History*, respectively.

Open systems and complexity theories explain how and why organizations experience typical business cycles and must adjust to routine fluctuations in the environment. Occasionally, this adjustment means transforming the system in response to disruptive fluctuations. Kodak and Sears are illustrative examples of long-standing companies whose failure to pivot resulted in their substantial falls from market dominance. Sears, once the world's largest retailer sought chapter 11 protection in 2018, soon after celebrating its 125th anniversary, for failure to adjust to the hyper-competitive online retail market. In 1888, George Eastman invented a meaningless word at the time, "Kodak" and established a company that would be a leader in film-based photography, a business dedicated to archiving memories (Kodak Company, n.d.). Kodak chose to stay with what it knew best, a film and camera company in lieu of pivoting toward the emerging technology of digital photography. Even though it invented the first digital camera, it filed for chapter 11 in 2012.

The history lessons from Sears and Kodak teach that leaders and managers must adopt systems-thinking to anticipate and adapt to changing environments. At the same time, this does not mean they have to abandon their histories and core values. On the contrary, their histories and core values become the foundation for managing change as they serve as the reference point(s) for ongoing midcourse corrections. Open systems and complexity theories equip organizational leaders and managers with a language and model to implement emerging planning, judiciously embrace change, and manage stability around their historical values and mission.

The logics of efficiency, sentiment, and complexity capture three historical stages of organizational development and corresponding facets of organizational activities. The picture remained incomplete in explaining both the ultimate driver and nonrational aspects of organizational life. As organizations and the study of organizations matured, institutional theory emerged to capture another major logic governing how and why tertiary pursuits become equally important as the organizations' core activities.

Institutional Theory – Meaning as the Ultimate Driver

President Calvin Coolidge stated in his 1925 address at the American Society of Newspaper Editors that "After all, the chief business of the American people is business." But what is often missed when Coolidge is cited as pro-business is why he made that statement. Coolidge in the same speech noted that business was a means to an end, and not an end in itself.

> We make no concealment of the fact that we want wealth, but there are many other things that we want very much more. We want peace and honor, and that charity which is so strong an element of all civilization. The chief ideal of the American people is idealism.

Coolidge captured that business is the path to advancing the highest ideas of society and in doing so, recognized that people, and by default organizations, take on symbolic justifications and corresponding features and activities.

Values matter and organizations adapt to accommodate additional and, at times, competing values. Philip Selznick (1919–2010), the founder of institutional theory proper, documented that many considerations converge over time to form the social structure of organizations, a process he labeled as institutionalization. It is a process "that happens to an organization over time, reflecting the organization's own distinctive history" (Selznick, 1957, p. 16). This history is:

> compounded of discernible and repetitive modes of responding to internal and external pressures. As the responses crystalize into definite patterns, a social structure emerges. The more fully developed its

social structure, the more will the organization become valued for itself, not as a tool but as an institutional fulfillment of group integrity and aspiration.

(Selznick, 1957, p. 16)

Organizational practices are values that are institutionalized when they take on rule-like status and establish expectations and norms that are taken for granted. Selznick observed that "to institutionalize" is "to infuse with value beyond the technical requirements of the task at hand" (p. 17).

Selznick's 1942–43 landmark study in the sociology of formal organizations revealed how and why tangential forces inevitably converge to mold organizations. He evaluated the creation and success of the Tennessee Valley Authority (TVA), a joint public-private enterprise authorized by Congress in May 1933. The TVA's "major powers – authority to construct dams, deepen the river channel, produce and distribute electricity and fertilizer – were delegated by Congress to a corporation administered by a three-man board" (Selznick, 1966, pp. 4–5). Today, the completely self-funded TVA manages one of the largest U.S. river systems and is the "U.S. largest public power provider that supplies electricity to nearly 10 million people across seven southeastern states, working in partnership with 153 local power companies" and manages one of the country's largest river systems (TVA, 2020).

The high stakes and broad scope of the TVA's establishment required cooperation among numerous farmers and local, regional, state, and national agencies. The challenge was to overcome territorial and interagency rivalries. The scale of activities required that cooperation among the numerous and diverse stakeholders be voluntary, consistent with the principles of democracy. A major insight from the TVA study was that organizations survive when they formally and informally adopt indispensable values and adapt practices to win the consent and participation of important stakeholders. Eventually, the cooptation of those values and practices took a life of their own to become institutionalized when they expand the organizational goals and mission. TVA emerged to becoming something different than what was originally intended (Ansar, 2018), demonstrably something better than expected, because of the cumulative influences of a variety of backstories that coopted the original mission and plans.

Meyer and Rowan (1977) expanded on Selznick's ideas in their seminal work, *Institutionalized Organizations: Formal Structure as Myth and Ceremony*, noting that:

Formal organizations are generally understood to be systems of coordinated and controlled activities that arise when work is embedded in complex networks of technical relations and boundary-spanning activities. But in modern societies formal organizations arise in highly institutionalized contexts. Professions, policies, and programs are created along with the products and services that they are understood to produce rationally.

(p. 340)

They established that "formal structures of many organizations in postindustrial society (Bell, 1973) dramatically reflect the myths of their institutional environments instead of the demands of their work activities" (p. 341). Organizations adopt practices beyond their core mission and function that typify expectations and themes in the industry (Schutz, 1962). Taken-for-granted assumptions become imprinted and prerequisites for organizational legitimacy, which explains why most universities offer resort-like amenities, business executives have disproportionately larger offices and salaries, medical doctors wear white coats when they see patients, schools have rows of desks, and state capital buildings have rotundas.

Selznick (1957) and Meyer and Rowan (1977) demonstrated that organizations are embedded in larger social environments. As a result, their actions are at the mercy of "multiple interpretations as people experience situations differently" (Bolman & Deal, 2017, p. 241). When dominant scripts reach critical mass, they become institutionalized to the degree that organizations must adopt and adhere to them. This explains why leaders and managers are now tasked to create thematized ambiances with accouterments that convey legitimacy and accommodate the diverse interests of their associated stakeholders.

Institutional theory captured how and why symbolic and "inefficient" activities are pursued and often become primary functions at considerable expense. For example, why invest in costly ceremonial U.S. Air Force, Army, Marine, and Navy bands, intercollegiate athletics, and commencement ceremonies? The U.S. military bands cost "$1.37 billion between 2012–2016 on salaries and allowances" and another "$157 million on operation costs, such as travel, instruments, and uniforms during the relatively the same period" (Olson, 2017). The NCAA (2020) reported that for the fiscal year 2019 that no Division I without football, Division II, and Division III institutions generated revenues that exceeded expenses and that only 25 athletic departments generated revenues that exceeded their expenses (NCAA, 2020). Washington State University's costs for commencement ceremonies at the end of spring, summer, and fall terms combined was $208,000 in 2015 (Hair, 2015). The University of Iowa reported a $45,000 deficit between costs associated with graduation from what the $75 graduation fee generated for the 2014 fiscal year, spending $634,288 (Charis-Carlson, 2015).

Military bands, university athletics, and commencement ceremonies have rich histories and provide inviting front porch views. They are also expensive costume balls that divert resources from their organizations' core functions. Mission creep is inevitable because of the convergence of value-driven backstories. Very few organizations are immune from larger community and societal values coopting to some degree their core mission, activities, and budget.

Not only does the "infusion of values" create mission creep, but it generates divided loyalties and competing reward systems. Kerr (1975) astutely observed that competing narratives abound in organizations and explained why organizations often espouse one thing and people do another. Kerr documented that when organizational and personal interests collide, the "zone of indifference" identified by Charles Barnard, personal narratives tend to win. Kerr explained that one reason the Vietnam War was a long war relative to WWII was a change in the incentive structure. WWII soldiers knew they would come home once the war was over. Vietnam soldiers knew they would return home when their tour of duty was over. Fighting to win a war is much different than fighting to survive one. Citing examples in politics, medicine, and education, Kerr demonstrated that leaders and managers often hope for one thing yet reward other things, such as hoping for teamwork but rewarding individual behavior and hoping for long-term growth but rewarding quarterly earnings.

The infusion of value and cooptation of organizational activities is manifested symbolically. For example, the profile on the obverse of the U.S. dime and the March of Dimes illustrates the power of symbols. In the first half of the 20th century, polio was one of the most feared diseases in the U.S. because it struck without warning, young children seemed especially vulnerable, and it left far too many people paralyzed (Oshinsky, 2005). President Franklin Roosevelt was diagnosed with polio in 1921 at the age of 39 and remained a paraplegic for the rest of his life. He founded the National Foundation of Infantile Paralysis (NFID) in 1938 to combat polio. On March 26, 1953, Dr. Jonas Salk announced that a vaccination against poliomyelitis had been developed, causing people to celebrate and lifting a dark cloud that closed schools, swimming pools, camps, and public gatherings during polio season.

Interestingly, not everyone was as celebratory at the announcement, for reasons best explained by institutional theory. It seemed strange to a young employee who showed up at his chapter NFID on March 26, 1953, that many of his colleagues were relatively forlorn at the announcement of the vaccine. When he inquired about the incongruous response, he was informed that they would be without a job now that the foundation had accomplished its one and only goal. The story as told by the former employee to one of the authors reveals that personal narratives seem to matter more than organizational narratives. The former employee recalled that rather than disband, the foundation adopted a new name and mission that would ensure it would remain a "flexible force" in public health.

The March of Dimes became the new name, the title of the NFID fundraising campaign that encouraged millions of people to spare a dime to alleviate polio. The new mission targeted multiple diseases affecting infants and children, avoiding the problem of extinction each time a new cure or vaccination was developed. It only seemed proper that Congress would memorialize FDR on the dime soon after his death on April 12, 1945.

Values matter, and when they are institutionalized, organizational missions are coopted. Organizations adapt by taking on activities that at one time were tangential to their core mission, but over time are now taken-for-granted and essential activities, even at considerable expense. For example, Budweiser has been raising and parading Clydesdales since 1933 that it would almost be an anathema if they were to stop.

An illustrative example of the use of symbols and traditions enthused with value becoming embedded in organizational ethos is the famed Lutine Bell. The Lutine Bell was part of a Lloyd's insured frigate carrying a cargo of gold and silver when it sank off the Dutch coast in 1799. The bell was recovered in 1859 and has hung in the Underwriting Rooms in the four different Lloyd's buildings since its recovery. The bell was traditionally rung to herald bad news – one ring when a vessel was loss, and good news – two rings when an overdue vessel arrived to port (Flower & Jones, 1974). Today the bell remains prominently displayed in Lloyd's and is wrung on rare ceremonial occasions. The bell is a clarion reminder of Lloyd's heritage of prompt payment of all valid claims, as in the case when the claim associated with sinking of the HMS Lutine was paid in full within two weeks, cementing Lloyd's reputation of integrity in the market insurance industry.

The Study and Practice of Good Leadership

As the task of leading organizations and institutions became increasingly complicated, another logic emerged. An additional framework was needed to explain how and why organizations and institutions with similar missions, structures, and workforces have very different work cultures and outcomes. The logics of efficiency, sentiment, complexity, and meaning stopped short in equipping people with the knowledge on how to best attend to and triage those logics. The study of leadership took on new import as people realized that with everything being equal across collectives that it was the quality of leadership that determined to what degree organizations were successful or unsuccessful.

James MacGregor Burns' 1978 seminal work, *Leadership*, marked the birth of leadership studies proper. While people were studying leadership prior to 1978, Burns was a catalyst in bringing leadership to the forefront and treating it as something more than management and administration. His historical work on leadership earned him the title "the father of leadership studies." He was the progenitor of formal academic programs in leadership studies and the burgeoning growth of leadership studies programs at institutions of higher education, distinct from the popular degrees in management and public administration. He was the co-founder of the International Leadership Association launched in 1999, the largest academic and professional association for leadership scholars and practitioners, distinct from the Academy of Management founded in 1936, the preeminent association for management and organizational scholars.

The study of history revealed another facet to understanding the collective and birthed the formal study of leadership, underscoring the didactic value of history. Specifically, Burns observed that leadership is a moral activity and much different than yielding power, emphatically noting that tyrants are not leaders. He also distinguished between two types of leaders in his thorough study of world leaders. Transactional leaders focus on quid pro exchanges within and across collectives to make things happen. In contrast, transforming leaders focus on unifying values and ideals to get people to engage above and beyond what they would normally do as moral agents to make the right things happen the right ways.

Bass (1985) and Bass and Avolio (1994) took the baton from Burns and evaluated what transformational leaders did to have transforming impacts on the collective. They identified and developed four components of transformational leadership. Transforming leaders are known for their:

1. Idealized influence – They are role models whose moral character make them winsome.
2. Inspirational motivation – They embody and clearly communicate compelling visions for moving forward.
3. Intellectual stimulation – They draw from deep wells of knowledge and understanding to solicit deeper thinking.
4. Individualized consideration – They authentically pay attention to developing others.

Transformational leadership is one of many different models on what makes for good leadership. Northouse's (2021) market-leading book, *Leadership: Theory and Practice* is in its 9th edition, reflecting the popularity and advancements in the study of leadership. Northouse notes that "Collectively, the research findings on leadership provide a picture of a process that is far more sophisticated and complex than the often-simplistic view presented in some of the popular books on leadership" (p. 1). Citing over 700 references, he documents the diverse and complementary approaches to and facets of leadership and demonstrates that it is a moral endeavor and type of influence based around a comprehensive set of traits, behaviors, skills, perspectives, and dispositions.

At its core, leadership addresses the nexuses of human aspirations, competences, diversity, nature, and relationships. Leadership is ultimately a moral crusade to make the right things happen the right way in and among collectives. Leadership explores and evaluates the stated and unstated values found in each collective and is what provides a unifying and governing logic on how to best operationalize and triage the other logics of efficiency, sentiment, complexity, and meaning. Leadership studies bring to the forefront that values matter. It is the values that determine the collective's goals, priorities, and the means by which those goals are pursued.

Leadership is both a moral influence and moral endeavor with correspondings sets of best practices. To be done well it requires that leaders be relatively astute philosophers, theologians, historians, social scientists, communicators, economists, strategists, and organizers. Leadership studies morphed into an interdisciplinary field of inquiry to help emerging and established leaders be competent in their value-laden roles as administrators, advocates, analysists, architects, catalysts, diplomats, managers, navigators, negotiators, performers, prophets, and servants (Bolman & Deal, 2017; Burns, 1978; Gardner, 1993; Shoup, 2016). History consistently reveals that bad leadership ruins good people and organizations, and that good leadership helps people and organizations thrive. The good news is that the study of leadership reveals that most of what makes for competent and value-driven leadership can be learned.

Conclusion

Formal collectives are heirs of their past. Since the Industrial Revolution organizations have inherited dominant sets of logics at different stages in their evolution to carry out their missions. These logics govern much of what happens in modern organizations. Organizations exist to provide quality products and services as efficiently as possible (e.g., rational systems). They rely on rational, emotional, and social individuals to develop and deliver those products and services (e.g., natural systems). To compete, they must astutely adjust to changes in the environment and balance the competing logics (e.g., open systems). To legitimately connect with diverse stakeholders, they must generate, communicate, and manage meaning (e.g., institutional theory). The respective systems were always present but took center stage at different times in the history and evolution of organizations proper. Each stage of development in the history of organizations expanded the role of the leader, necessitating the study of what makes for good leadership. The field of leadership studies emerged to discover and teach best practices for leaders to make the right things happen the right way, recognizing that leadership is ultimately moral influence over what collectives do and how they perform.

Notes

1. ASAE was founded in 1920 and serves 46,000 association executives and represents 7,400 organizations (ASAE, 2019).
2. This does not mean formal organizations did not exist prior to Weber and Taylor. Feudal and military empires had formal hierarchical structures in place, but such structures were limited in number and scope.
3. The Hawthorne Study resulted in what became known eponymously as the Hawthorne Effect, noting that people tend to change their behavior in response to being observed.
4. As early as the 1600s organizational leaders had to navigate open systems, but at a more limited scale than modern society.
5. Flower and Jones (1974) noted that Lloyd developed a network of reporters at principal ports to send and receive timely news as a means to attract additional merchant leaders to his business. In 1696, Lloyd started publishing his reports in his *Lloyd's News* for his patrons, thus establishing his coffee shop as the "nerve-centre of shipping news" (p. 24) that attracted ship owners and merchants to his coffee house.

References

Ansar, A. (2018). The fate of ideas in the real world: A long view on Philip Selznick's classic on the Tennessee Valley Authority (TVA). *International Journal of Project Management, 36*, 385–395.

ASAE. (2019). About ASAE. *ASAE Center.* www.asaecenter.org/about-us.

Balkin, J. (2020). *The cycles of constitutional time.* Oxford University Press.

Barabási, A., & Bonabeau, E. (2003). Scale-free networks. *Scientific American, 288*(5), 60–69. www.jstor.org/stable/26060284

Barnard, C. (1938). *The Functions of the executive.* Harvard University Press.

Barnard, C. (1948). *Organization and management.* Harvard University Press.

Bass, B. M. (1985). *Leadership and performance beyond expectation.* Free Press.

Bass, B. M., & Avolio, B. J. (1994). *Improving organizational effectiveness through transformational leadership.* Sage Publications, Inc.

Bell, D. (1973). *The coming of post-industrial society.* Basic Books.

Bolman, L. G., & Deal T.E. (2017). *Reframing organizations: Artistry, choice, and leadership.* John Wiley & Sons.

Burns, J. M. (1978). *Leadership.* Harper& Row.

Busch, L. (2017). Herbert hoover and the construction of modernity. *Journal of Innovation Economics & Management,22*(1), 29–55. doi.org/10.3917/jie.pr1.i

Charis-Carlson, J. (2015). Where does the money from the graduation fee go? *Iowa City Press-Citizen.* www.press-citizen.com/story/news/education/college/2015/05/17/college-graduation-fees-expenses/27501669/.

Coolidge, C. (1925, December 6). *The press under a free government.* Address before the American Society of Newspaper Editors, Washington, D.C.

Drucker, P. (1995). Introduction. In P. Graham (Ed.), *Mary Parker Follett: Prophet of management* (pp. 1–9). Harvard Business School Press.

Flower, R., & Jones, M. (1974). *Lloyd's of London: An illustrated history.* Hastings House, Publishers.

Follett, M. P. (1924). *The creative experience.* Green and Co.

Gardner, J. (1993). *On leadership.* Free Press.

Gibb, D. E. W. (1924). Recent developments in Lloyd's. *Harvard Business Review, 2*(3), 345–353.

Gilbreth, F. B., & Careym E. G. (1948). *Cheaper by the dozen.* Thomas Y. Crowell Co.

Hair, C. (2015). Voices: What do your graduation fees actually pay for? *USA Today*.www.usatoday.com/story/college/2015/03/30/voices-what-do-your-graduation-fees-actually-pay-for/37401987/

Harris, J. (2001). *General introduction.* In J. Harris (Ed.) & M. Hollis (Trans.), Tönnies: Community and Civil Society (Cambridge Texts in the History of Political Thought, pp. Ix–Xxx). Cambridge University Press.

Haueter, N. (2017). *A history of insurance.* Swiss Re.

Kerr, S. (1975). On the folly of rewarding A, while hoping for B. *Academy of Management Journal,18,* 769–783.

Kodak Company. (n.d.). *George Eastman history.* www.kodak.com/en/company/page/george-eastman-history

McNally, J. J. (2018). Functions of the executive. *Academy of Management Learning & Education,17*(1), 112–114. doi.org/10.5465/amle.2017.0420

Metcalf, H., & Urwick, H. (Eds). (1942). *Dynamic administration: The collected papers of Mary Parker Follett.* Harper and Brothers.

Meyer, J., & Rowan, B. (1977). Institutionalized organizations: Formal structure as myth and ceremony. *American Journal of Sociology, 83*(2), 340–363. www.jstor.org/stable/2778293.

NCAA. (2020). Finances of Intercollegiate Athletics. *NCAA.* www.ncaa.org/about/resources/research/finances-intercollegiate-athletics.

Northouse, P. (2021). *Leadership: Theory and practice* (9th ed.). Sage Publications.

Odell, G. T. (1925). Herbert hoover: Super business man. *The Nation, 121,* 325–327.

Olson, W. (2017). GAO: Did $1.5 billion in military music boost morale? *Stars and Stripes.* www.stripes.com/news/gao-did-1-5-billion-in-military-music-boost-morale-1.482382

Oshinsky, D. M. (2005). *Polio: An American story.* Oxford University Press.

Roethlisberger, F. J., & Dickson, W. J. (1939/1961). *Management and the worker.* Harvard University Press.

Schlesinger, A. M., Jr. (1986/1999). *The cycles of American history.* Macmillan Co.

Schlesinger, A. M., Sr. (1949). *Paths to the present. Episodes of liberal reform and conservative reaction.* Macmillan Co.

Schutz, A. (1962). *The problem of social reality: Collected papers I.* Mar-tinus Nijhoff.

Selznick, P. (1957). *Leadership in administration: A sociological interpretation.* Harper & Row.

Selznick, P. (1966). *TVA and the grass roots: A study in the sociology of formal organization.* Harper & Row.

Shoup, J. (2016). Leadership, organizational, and institutional studies: Reconciling and teaching competing perspectives. *Journal of Leadership Education,15,* 167–182.

Shoup, J., & Studer, S. (2010). *Leveraging chaos: The mysteries of leadership and policy revealed.* Rowman & Littlefield Education.

Taylor, F. W. (1911). *The principles of scientific management.* Harper & Bros.

Lloyd's act. (1871). The Corporation of Lloyd's.

Tönnies, F. (1887/2001). *Community and civil society* (J. Harris & M. Hollis, Trans.). Cambridge University Press (Original work published 1887).

TVA. (2020). *Annual report, fiscal year 2020.*www.tva.com/annualreport

Weber, M. (1905). *The protestant ethic and the spirit of capitalism.* Pantianos Classics.

Weber, M. (1922/1978). *Economy and society.* University of California Press.

Williams, R., & Drew, M. (2012). *Pendulum: How past generations shape our present and predict our future.* Vanguard Press.

4 History and Contemporary Lessons for Leaders

Introduction

As demonstrated in the first three chapters, history is didactic. It is more than a chronology of facts and milestones, although timetables are foundational for constructing usable narratives. History is more than crafting relevant stories, although necessary for granting people and events their due import. History is more than a tribute on what to emulate and or indictment on what to avoid, although candid commentaries are instructive. History is ultimately "philosophy teaching by examples"[1] and designed to make people wise.[2]

History in general and of individual organizations are unique tutors and mentors. Cicero (1860) noted in his *De Oratore* that history is life's teacher. Historical narratives uniquely teach and equip business leaders and managers with perspectives to:

- Develop endearing emotional and social intelligences and cultural knowledge.
- Shape and promote meaningful and relevant organizational identity, loyalty, and pride around cherished values and organizational milestones.
- Leverage the past to navigate organizational dilemmas, manage uncertainty, anticipate the future.
- Cultivate deeper appreciation and sense of gratitude for the present and less of a taken-for-granted attitude of accumulated blessings.
- Honor important individuals and milestones and transmit important values to the next generation.

Doing Organizational History

The practice of doing organizational histories has changed significantly since the Renaissance. Wadhwani et al. (2018) noted that prior to the Enlightenment and until relatively recent, history was studied and taught for what it could teach. They documented that:

DOI: 10.4324/9781003100171-4

History was considered "useful" because the past offered a reservoir of cases and examples that served as analogies pertinent to problems in the present, an understanding that persisted through the medieval and Renaissance periods. Those leaders with knowledge of historical events and figures could draw on these analogies as a guide for decision-making in the present. From this perspective, history was understood not primarily as a representation of the past, but rather as a rhetorical and didactical tool that provided relevant, useful, and applicable plots and morals that could serve strategic purposes in the present (Grethlein, 2011; Rüsen, 1987; Mordhorst & Schwarzkopf, 2017).

(p. 1665)

The Enlightenment's "professionalization of history" focused on the "past itself as itself" so as to provide a more objective telling of what transpired (Wadhwani et al., 2018). The study of history came to lack a "so what" telos beyond the voyeuristic curiosity of what people thought and did back then. The corrective return to "the mobilization of the past in the present" for historians emerged in part out of revaluating the value of history for modern audiences and, in part, of out of the recognition that "history is a uniquely humanist form of knowledge that continually integrates facts about the past with the values, desires, and interpretive processes of actors in the present" (p. 1666).

For organizational leaders, the relatively recent reclaiming of history's didactive value is now informing the study of organizations (McDonald, 1996; Clark & Rowlinson, 2004; Rowlinson, 2013). The significance of this historical turn prompted the editors of the Academy of Management Review and the Journal of Organization Studies to initiate special issues – *History & Organization Studies* (2016) and *Uses of the Past in Organization Studies* (2018), respectively. The Centre for Business History in Stockholm and the American Business History Center are additional evidence that organizational histories are proving to be valued resources for both the organizational scholars and practitioners. The History Factory has been in business for more than 40 years and as posted on their website landing page, they have helped an impressive array of companies leverage their heritage to shape their futures.

History as a Personal Tutor

History uniquely exposes the mind and heart to the joys and travails of life, cultivates an empathy and appreciation for others, reveals how the world works, and paints a picture of what matters most in life. In that regard, history is a crash course for increasing one's emotional and social intelligences and cultural awareness, the mindsets that matter more than other native abilities when it comes to leading.

Emotional (EQ) and social (SQ) intelligences are what get people promoted and equip them to be better leaders, even if they are not the smartest members on the team. Leaders unable to manage their emotions with a modicum of intelligence eventually leave a wake of destruction in their paths. Leaders unable to intelligently play well with others and to "read the room"[3] are excluded from the parties. Intellectual and technical abilities are important, but they are what Goleman (1998) called "the threshold capabilities," entry-level requirements for any profession. They are necessary acquired abilities, but they are not sufficient to equip people to be long-term guests at the leadership table.

Daniel Goleman documented in his books, *Emotional Intelligence (1995)* and *Social Intelligence: The New Science of Human Relationships* (2006) the plethora of advantages that come with EQ and SQ and the disadvantages when they are lacking. Goleman (2006) provided an illustrative and compelling story on the power of EQ and SQ.

> During the early days of the second American invasion of Iraq, a group of soldiers set out for a local mosque to contact the town's chief cleric. Their goal was to ask his help in organization of relief supplies. But a mob gathered, fearing the soldiers were coming to arrest their spiritual leader or destroy the mosque, a holy shrine.
>
> Hundreds of devout Muslims surrounded the soldiers, waving their hands in the air and shouting, as they pressed toward the heavily armed platoon. The commanding officer, Lieutenant Colonel Christopher Hughes, thought fast.
>
> Picking up a loudspeaker, he told his soldiers to "take a knee," meaning to kneel on one knee. Next he ordered them to point their rifles toward the ground. Then his order was: "Smile."
>
> (p. 3)

Goleman described next that the crowd's mood was transformed, and the situation went quickly from hostile to calm, thanks to a "quick-witted move" that "was the culmination of split-second social calculations" (p. 4). Lt. Colonel Hughes' quick thinking was made possible because of his higher levels of EQ and SQ.

Goleman (1998) identified EQ as the ability to:

- Recognize and understand one's own emotions (self-awareness),
- Control one's emotions (self-regulation),
- Passionately pursue goals with energy and persistence (motivation),

- Understand and consider others' feelings (empathy), and
- Manage relationships and build endearing and enduring networks (social-awareness).

Goleman (2006) acknowledged that while he initially folded SQ in his EQ model, he realized that SQ was worthy as a standalone theory because of its focus on what transpires when people interact. He broke SQ down to two broad categories with corresponding abilities.

Social Awareness (sensing)

- Primal empathy – feeling with others
- Attunement – active listening
- Social cognition – understanding how the social world works

Social Facility (fruitful interactions based upon accurate sensing)

- Synchrony – rhythmic interactions with others
- Self-presentation – selective authenticity
- Influence – positive impact on the social interactions and outcomes
- Concern – care and kindness toward others.

Emotional and social intelligences (ESQ) allow people to be more accurately aware of themselves, others, and situations. Socio-emotional intelligence equips people to effectively self-regulate and practice and empathy. As a result, people with high ESQ are more prone to keep their emotions in check and make others feel listened to and valued. They are better able to read people and the room so as to act wisely when building cohesive teams and making consequential decisions. A variety of studies have confirmed that socio-emotionally intelligent leaders are better able to manage conflict, promote higher levels of employee engagement and productivity, and increase employee and customer retention and loyalty. Naznin (2013) also demonstrated a strong correlation between EQ and transformational leadership behavior. ESQ's endearing qualities allow leaders to be finely attuned to people and situations (Goleman & Boyatzis, 2008).

The good news is that while EQ and SQ may come easier for some, it can be developed through learning, reflection, and practice (Devis-Rozental, 2018). Social learning theory established that role-models, role-playing, and social interactions are especially effective in cultivating socio-emotional intelligence (Bandura, 1977; Vygotsky, 1978). History, especially historical novels and biographies, provides readers vicarious experiences with an array of role-models at different stages of development and real-life role plays in dynamic social interactions for readers to reflect upon.

Good histories allow readers to reflexively put themselves in the shoes of others (empathy), understand dynamic forces shaping events and peoples' experiences, thoughts, and feelings (social and situational awareness), and experience consequences of beliefs and habits of relating (motivations, synchrony, self-presentation, and influence). History is a shortcut to experience and allows the inner historians in everyone to uniquely interact with, experience, and reflect on multiple lifetimes of people and events in one lifetime.

Just as having a sense of history promotes personal and social maturity, it is also an important source of cultural capital, a term coined by French philosopher Pierre Bourdieu. In his, *The Forms of Capital*, Bourdieu (1986) stated that "the social world is accumulated history" (p. 241) that yields different forms of capital – economic (accumulation of physical resources that are directly convertible to money), social (accumulation of social connections and obligations that afford privileges), and cultural (accumulation of valued knowledge and habits that reproduce social values and structures). For Bourdieu, while there are correlations among social and economic capital, his focus was on transmission and reproduction of cherished values, the useful passing on of certain dispositions and habits among groups of people. Bourdieu described the social stratification of preferences and taste to demonstrate that social classes take on deep distinctions that set them apart and correspondingly give them relative advantages or disadvantages in larger society. For example, there are different sets of dispositions, tastes, and manners among those in highbrow, middlebrow, and lowbrow communities and societies evident by generally adopted preferences for music and cuisine among geographical and social groups.

Expanding on Bourdieu, cultural capital refers to levels of shared understanding of events and people that have come to take on special significance in both their original and modern contexts and are used to strategically engage others. Ultimately, cultural capital can be a resource to leverage the social conscience of society and promote the highest ideas and values of humanity.[4] For example, Martin Luther King Jr.'s "I Have a Dream" speech delivered on August 28, 1963, to a crowd of 250,000, leveraged accumulated history in a way that made the speech itself historically significant and recognized for its greatness. The speech was profoundly strengthened with allusions to important history, specifically the Gettysburg Address, the Emancipation Proclamation, the Declaration of Independence, the U.S. Constitution, Shakespeare, and the Bible when it was poetically delivered under the watchful eye of Abraham Lincoln at the Lincoln Memorial (Pruitt, 2021).

To this day the words "I have a dream" evoke certain emotions and remembrances and inspire people to strive for a future of unprecedented "brotherhood" when people will "not be judged by the color of their skin but by the content of their character" in "an oasis of freedom and justice" where "freedom rings" perpetually. Any reference to the four words, "I have a dream" should automatically take people back to Martin Luther King Jr.'s message and, however momentarily, cause them to relive a bit of important history and empathetically strive to be better people today and make the world better for their children.

In a similar fashion to Martin Luther King Jr., leaders and managers can call up cultural scripts and use of historical allusion to create "digital moments" that uniquely connect, provide direction, and promote meaning with stakeholders, assuming shared understandings of history. Terms and phrases like Stonewalling, Pyrrhic victory, Janus effect, a Benedict Arnold or Casanova, Waterloo and Watergate events, "Remember the Alamo," Spartan conditions, storming the Bastille, the Midas touch, a Kodak moment, Big Brother is watching, Machiavellian, A Luddite, Damascus road experience, a White Elephant Gift, "Let them eat cake," the Ides of March, and "Et tu, Brute?" are shortcut expressions rich with historical overtones, which, when cited, efficiently provide important perspectives for the moment.[5]

Every word and phrase has its historical context and significance (Almond, 1985). For example, the phrase "A-1" represents "the very best" and originated from Lloyd's of London when they "started a register of ships and shipments in which the condition of the ships and their cargo was noted. The ships were graded by letter; the cargoes by number. "A" meant that the ship itself was perfect; "1" that the cargo was likewise perfect" (Almond, 1985, p. 9).

While some knowledge of the past might be considered useful only for trivial pursuit competitions, certain histories create and generate cultural understandings and serve as the foundation of cultural capital. When used appropriately, historical allusions:

- Create a sense of affinity and kinship with the collective identity.
- Efficiently and creatively convey important values and ideas that would otherwise take too long to explain.
- Invite others to evaluate themselves in relation to the people and events being alluded to.
- Prompt personal growth and valued social action.

Knowledge of history-at-large develops emotional, social, and cultural intelligences. Knowledge of history at the local and organizational levels equips leaders and managers with necessary understandings to create stand-alone advantages in their competitive marketplaces.

Organizational History as Identity

Leaders and managers consistently use narrative to establish and maintain their corporate cultures, identities, and images (Hatch & Schultz, 2002). They are sensemakers and sensegivers who use narratives to make associations that endear stakeholders to themselves and their organizations (Shoup & Hinrichs, 2019; Besharov & Brickson, 2016). History at large and organizations' individual histories provide the anchors for compelling identity narratives that, when properly crafted, solicit and sustain inward and outward relational commitments (Oertel & Thommes, 2018; Suddaby et al., 2016; Zundel et al., 2016).

More often than not, a firm's identity narrative is firmly rooted in the founder(s)'s vision and values (Basque & Langley, 2018). Such sentiment was captured by Tim Cook, CEO of Apple, when he stated in a 2016 interview,

> From my point of view, Steve [Jobs] – his spirit will always be the DNA of the company. He embodied who we are. It was his vision that Apple should make the best products, and it was his vision that they should enrich people's lives. Lots of other things will change with Apple, but that will never change.
> (Balakrishnan, 2016; as cited in Basque & Langley, 2018, p. 1686)

Basque and Langley (2018) cited various research that documented when corporate identities are tied to the ideas of their founders that the respective histories provide several advantages, especially through changing times. They described "organization identity work" as "the way in which an organization's top manager mobilize discursive elements in their communications to promote conceptions of identity likely to resonate with their audiences" (p. 1688). They noted that rhetorical uses of history are important, but are often underutilized organizational assets that can uniquely "draw on and orient collective memories to establish organizational identity and to stimulate identification (member-ship) from stakeholders" (p. 1668).

Lasewicz (2015) noted that "the use of heritage in corporate identity mixes so powerful that sometimes companies – in lieu of utilizing their own heritage – incorporate broader national heritage themes into their corporate or brand identities" (p. 73). This is especially useful for organizations in their early stages since they have yet to forge their own identity. Foster et al., (2011) attributed the early and sustained success of the restaurant chain Tim Hortons in part to the company's association of itself with two important Canadian institutions. Tim Horton was a hockey legend, and the chain chose early on in its history to incorporate schematic narratives from Canadian hockey and military to make social memory an asset in their business plan. Identifying Tim Hortons with Canadian history and heritage shaped expectations and facilitated instant bonding among consumers.

In a similar tradition, St. Croix Knitcraft, doing business in the high-end apparel industry since 1960, adopted its current name from the counsel of Mr. Stanley Marcus (of Neiman-Marcus) based upon his sense of history (and geography). Mr. Bernie Brenner, the founder of St. Croix, recalls Mr. Marcus stating in a sales meeting:

> Bernie . . . I love your product. It's absolutely great. But your label is not right . . . . Weren't there a lot of French immigrants who settled in your country? You need a French sounding name like some of the nice rivers in your part of the country. Isn't there a St. Croix River? At that point the "Mr. Knitter" name on the knitwear labels were replaced with St. Croix to reflect the hardworking river and heritage of the people residing in that part of Minnesota.
>
> (St. Croix Collections, n.d.)

Organizational identities are inexplicably linked to their pasts. They are unique resources that when properly leveraged can coalesce stakeholders, clarify communication, facilitate learning, reinforce identity, streamline communications, and guide strategic planning (Zundel et al., 2016; Lasewicz, 2015). But more importantly they "forge identities and actively manage the perceptions of internal and external audiences" (Zundel et al., 2016, p. 212). Organizational identities are expressions of their individual and collective culture, which in turn provide the narratives for their organizational images (Hatch & Schultz, 2002). Organizational members develop their identities "in relation to who they perceive they are" and manage their image "in relation to what others say about them" (Hatch & Schultz, 2002, p. 1000). Rhetorical histories bring the past forward to provide didactic reference points to establish and maintain identities around core values.

Rhetorical histories are the authentic and strategic invoking of the usable past. They are the scripts for the sensemaking and sensegiving stories leaders use to confer legitimacy on past, present, and future activities and create organizational identity, loyalty, and competitiveness. Rhetorical histories are unique to each organization and can be used strategically to stand out from competitors and display their values and commitment to those values (Suddaby et al., 2016).

Smith and Steadman (1981) noted in their Harvard Business Review article, *Present Value of Corporate History*, that organizational histories are an unexploited resource, in part because of previous poor use and reputation of history. But when done properly, they better equip leaders and managers to direct change, help stakeholders cope with change by connecting the present experiences to a larger history, learn from previous successes and failures, and transmit cherished values. While most business and organizational leaders are not able to host their own museums or on-site historians, they can think historically and gradually capture and craft their own rhetorical histories.

Suddaby et al. (2016) identified ways that leaders and managers can engage in the "complex interactions of organizational identity, rhetorical history, and collective memory" (p. 307), which they refer to as re-membering. They intentionally separated the prefix from the root with a hyphen to

> reinforce the observation that *memory and membership are common social constructions* and that *identification, or the creation of a sense of commonality and belonging, is inherently connected to and dependent upon the strategic and creative narrative reconstruction in a given community*. [italics original].
>
> (pp. 298–299)

There are the formal re-membering activities from hosting in-house museums, commissioning corporate histories and biographies, retelling of paradigmatic stories at official gatherings, and strategic use of organizational spaces and brand logos. The informal activities of re-membering happen through casual conversations on the shop floor and around the proverbial watercooler, which are hopefully informed by formal re-membering scripts.

Smith and Steadman (1981) encouraged leaders and managers to think historically in their active routines by following some of the formal rules of the discipline consistent with the characteristics of history described in chapter two.

- See and explain the flow of events as a process over time, not just a sequence of isolated events.
- Approach the past with a sense of surprise – that is, regard events and decisions as uncertain and thus recapture them unaffected by their outcomes.
- Treat any part of the past on its own terms and in ways that would have been comprehensible to people of that period. (Our natural tendency is to distort the past by reading it in light of our own experiences and values.)
- Understand particular historical problems or episodes in their contemporary social, intellectual, political, and economic contexts.

(p. 170)

There are organizations that capture organizational histories for those who are reluctant or pressed for time to craft their own. The History Factory has been in business since 1979 and as stated on their website, they have assisted Fortune 500 clients to "advance business agendas, raise brand awareness, engage and inspire employees, and spark growth" by leveraging their pasts. They also provide on their website vignettes and articles that support their claims that organizational leaders who take advantage of their collective memories by showcasing defining events, people, and stories experience competitive advantages.

One of many examples of leaders and managers thinking historically and demonstrating that the usable past matters is story about Adidas uncovering its history to make for an enviable comeback story (Iglesias et al., 2020). First, the didactic backstory, Adidas and Puma are two shoe factories located in Herzogenaurach Germany on separate ends of town that were formally founded by brothers Adi and Rudolf Dassler, respectively. Adi, a versatile athlete, realized that shoes customized to the different running sports would provide competitive advantages in the corresponding arenas. He crafted field-tested athletic shoes that would become the footwear of many Olympians in the 1928 and 1936 summer Olympic games, including Jesse Owens, a four-time U.S. gold medalist in the Berlin games. Rudolph joined Adi in the initial years and together they formed the Dassler Brothers Shoe Factory in 1924. In 1948 the brothers had an epic fallout that resulted in them going their separate ways. They divided the assets, employees, and the town and established their own athletic shoe companies. They were lifelong competitors who did not speak to each other up to their deaths for reasons still shrouded in speculation. Adidas (Adi) and Puma (Rudolf) were born out of competition and became multi-billion dollars revenue companies.

When Adi Dassler died in 1978 the company changed strategies and direction, eventually diluting the band identity and product quality to the point that the Dassler family sold the business in 1990 (Iglesias et al., 2020). In preparation of the sale, the CEO invited two former Nike managers to advise on the strategic turnaround needed to better position the company for prospective buyers. During the tour of the company, specifically at the small museum, one of the consults had an epiphany – "It only took about five minutes in the museum before I realized that these people had nothing but a gold mine in their hands and they really had no idea what they had" (Iglesias, 2020, p. 54). At that point, they started to imagine "how they could leverage Adidas' history and the founder's philosophy to inspire a new corporate brand strategy that could revamp its competitive positioning and steer the company forward" (p. 54).

They were surprised to discover that the important history of enhancing athletic performance was lost in the collective memory of the employees and that Adi's "copious notebooks, containing 50 years of ideas and sketches" and extensive shoe collection were hidden in storage (Iglesias, 2020, p. 54).

They set out to discover and leverage Adidas' former history. They outlined a new strategy that resulted in a renewed sense of pride. The senior design director expressed, "it was back to the roots, but connecting it to the values of the brand and the values of Adi Dassler" (p. 55). The marketing director shared that "As funny as it sounds, I remember the goosebumps I had when they [the consultants] for the first time made me and others really, really proud of where we work, and understand what a great brand it is" (p. 55). The new strategy worked and, as documented by Iglesias et al. (2020), the new focus made Adidas cool again and helped Adidas' sales reach €5.3 billion in 1999, ten years after it was near bankruptcy.

History as a Window

Janus, a god from Roman mythology, has two opposing faces so that he can look at the past and future simultaneously. Accordingly, he is the guardian of doors, gates, and roads. He is also called *Janitor* from which the appellation for those who have keys to the facilities is derived. The month of January is named after him to mark new beginnings (Mythology, 1833, p. 114). Janus is the symbol for transitions and reflects the wisdom of knowing the past to judiciously prepare for the future. In that spirit, Seaman and Smith (2012), state "that leaders with no patience for history are missing a vital truth: A sophisticated understanding of the past is a most powerful tool for shaping the future" (p. 46).

The continuity of the past with the future in relation to progress was also noted by the Spanish-American philosopher George Santayana. He wrote that retaining valuable experiences is necessary to advance, to move beyond collective infancy, hence his famous aphorism, "Those who cannot remember the past are condemned to repeat it" (Santayana, 1905, p. 172). Unfortunately, even with knowledge of the past, people and organizations are still destined to repeat history at some scale because the values and patterns that shaped the past are still at play in the present. Fortunately, complexity theory referenced in chapter three provides a lens which leaders and managers can understand the patterns of the past and better anticipate and mediate forthcoming trends revealed in the patterns of time (Shoup & Studer, 2010).

A long view of history reveals that while human progress appears sequential, it is a cyclical pattern around a perennial set of universal values and corresponding competition to be first among equals. Chapter three provided a sequential history of organizational theories and practices and highlighted the emerging and competing logics driving organizational activities. This section presents a cyclical orientation of history to demonstrate how the dominant logics keep the social systems in relative balance or equilibrium. A brief history of management fads reveals that history does repeat itself as a repackaging of the old under new labels. Reoccurring fads are how systems correct themselves. A long view of history reveals that there is not really anything new under the sun (Ecclesiastes), just inevitable seasonal apparitions of the past.

As stated in chapter three, researchers in the physical and social sciences concurrently discovered around the same time the hidden architecture governing all dynamic systems. Organizations are social systems embedded in other social systems, making them complex adaptive systems (CAS). All CAS survive by maintaining equilibrium around defining reference points. The human body is a system of systems that experiences ongoing feedback to maintain desired equilibrium points in the circulatory, digestive, endocrine, lymphatic, nervous, muscular, and exocrine systems and collectively as a whole. When the body temperature gets too high in relation to an optimal reference point (98.2 F for the average adult) the systems collaborate and make the necessary changes or corrections to bring the system back to its desired equilibrium point.

The physical plant of an organization does something similar when regulating the temperature of buildings and workspaces. When a room gets too cool, the thermometer (feedback mechanism) sends a message to the heating, ventilation, and air conditioning unit (HVAC) to send additional heat. Once the room reaches the desired temperature (the equilibrium reference point, or what complexity refers to as a strange attractor), the thermometer sends a message to the HVAC to stop sending heat until needed. Throughout the day in response to what is happening in the room and larger environment, the HVAC system continuously turns the heat off and on (feedback loop), making regular changes, to keep the room temperature at the set reference point.

Social systems have their equivalent strange attractors and feedback mechanisms to remain relatively stable. Social systems have multiple strange attractors, in contrast to the single reference point in the HVAC example referenced above. The strange attractors in social systems are the dominant values or logics. The ongoing feedback informed corrections create patterns at the macro and micro levels of society. In a free market economy, Adam Smith (1776) called this process the invisible hand in market economy. The local economy maintains relative equilibrium through countless exchanges to financially benefit individuals and the collective.

In history at large, the most basic strange attractors are survival, peace and freedom, and human thriving. Collectives in the form of families, states, and nations do what is necessary to survive. People ban together by familial, ethnic, and/or national tribes to enhance their survival and if deemed necessary, engage in conflicts at small (sibling rivalry) and large scales (war) to protect themselves and have access to cherished resources. Yet, survival without social contracts for peace there would be anarchy and little time and freedom to pursue the cherished goals, hence the desire and goal for social harmony and world peace. Individuals and tribes ultimately want to survive so that they can thrive in whatever fashion they are so inclined, but only to the degree that those pursuits do not encroach on the inclinations and needs of others.

The U.S. Declaration of Independence captured on paper three dominant and competing unalienable Rights – Life (survival), Liberty (peace and freedom), and the pursuit of Happiness (human thriving at the individual and collective level).[6] The rally call of the French Revolution – Liberty, Equality, Fraternity likewise captured the cherished values and the implied tension of balancing individual and collective rights. The Constitution of the People's Republic of China balances equality and unity as their strange attractors to achieve collective survival, peace, and prosperity. As stated in the Preamble:

> The People's Republic of China is a unitary multi-national State created jointly by the people of all nationalities. Socialist relations of equality, unity and mutual assistance have been established among the nationalities and will continue to be strengthened. In the struggle to safeguard the unity of nationalities. . . . The State will do its utmost to promote the common prosperity of all nationalities.

A long view of history exposes that keeping equilibrium around the strange attractors is messy, yet relatively revealing about what the future holds. When one value becomes too dominant at the expense of others, the other values will cause the system to eventually become the first among equals for that period. Hence, state, national, and world leaders govern to balance the competing expectations associated with the dominant strange attractors at the individual and collective levels. An extreme form of correction is war and explains why regional conflict will always occupy past and future histories, hopefully not on the scale of WWI and WWII. Conflicts at the family, regional, national, and global levels are inevitable when their individual and collective quests to survive and thrive pushes up against the individual and collective harmony and peace.

Understanding the hidden architecture of CAS equips parents, managers, mayors, governors, and presidents to anticipate and potentially temper extreme self-corrections and judiciously intervene when necessary. The social system works well on paper, but because there are winners and losers, intended and unintended consequences, and potential for corrupt leaders with each correction, the system can feel chaotic to those with a short view of history.

The primary source of feedback in social CAS is the people, and the primary mechanism for regulating the feedback are the leaders. Just as the steersman of a sailboat is constantly making midcourse corrections to the tiller to keep the boat on tack in response to the wind and other objects in the water, so leaders and managers make ongoing adjustments and correction in response to feedback, being judicious to not overcorrect and get off-course or capsize. The

Greek word for steersman is governor and explains why state chief executive officers have inherited that appellation. Governors, like leaders and managers, must judiciously and skillfully balance multiple and competing interests, keeping them first among equals at different times to keep the system running smoothly around desired equilibrium points (Shoup & Studer, 2010).

At a smaller scale, organizations compete to survive and ultimately thrive by cooperating with others. They attend to the strange attractors at large in the affairs of humanity and their respective manifestations at the organizational level. Organizations thrive to the degree leaders and manager focus on efficiencies (rational system), attend to personnel's personal needs (natural systems), and anticipate physical and existential opportunities and threats in the larger environment of the others (open systems).

A glimpse of the emergence of management fads reveals how dominant values reemerge as ongoing correctives. Contemporary fads are iterations of previous ones couched in new terminology. While there are precipitating causes to how and why firms embrace fads, their respective appearances are ultimately part of a larger pattern (Gibson & Tesone, 2001; Piazza & Abrahamson, 2020). Business fads are reiterations of voices from the past from the dominant organizational logics identified in chapter three. Below are just a few examples:

Rational and Structural – logic of efficiency

- 1987 – Six Sigma (Cano et al., 2012) is an extreme version of Max Weber and Frederick Taylor.

Natural and Human Relations – logic of sentiment

- 1990 – Employee Engagement (Kahn & Fellows, 2013),
- 2001 – Now, Discover Your Strengths (Buckingham & Clifton, 2001), and
- 2002 – Five Dysfunctions of a Team (Lencioni, 2002)

are reincarnations of Elton Mayo, Mary Follet, and Chester Barnard.
Open Systems – logic of complexity

- 1996 – The Balanced Scorecard (Kaplan & Norton, 1996),
- 2018 – The Agile Leader: How to Create an Agile Business in the Digital Age (Hayward, 2018), and
- 2004 – Blue Ocean Strategy (Kim & Mauborgne, 2004)

are reminders that organizations attend to multiple bottom lines in an uncertain environment.

Gibson and Tesone (2001) argued that leaders and managers would do well to discern if the current fad fits with their organization at that moment in their history. The larger lesson for leaders and managers is to understand why fads come and resist adopting the latest one in management because it happens to be trendy. Their advice is to hold on to what is at the core of the different fads and to lead from multiple perspectives and frames.

Bolman and Deal (2017) demonstrate the soundness of that advice in their *Reframing Organizations: Artistry, Choice, and Leadership*, now in its 6th edition. They identify the structural, human resource, political, and symbolic frames for understanding how and why organizations function the way that they do. Each frame represents the logics from the rational, natural, open, and institutional logics outlined in chapter three, respectively. Bolman and Deal encourage leaders to attend to each frame as analysts and architects (structural), catalysts and servants (human relations), advocates and negotiators (political), and prophets and poets (symbolic).

History at the macro and micro levels is marked by periods of time when a set of values take precedence over others. There are stable patterns in history because of dominant sets of values that keep the system in check. While history is relatively stable, it is also emerging. Emergence is another concept common to all CAS. There are tipping points in history, such as the American, French, and Chinese Revolutions. There are tipping points in the life of organizations, most notable are advances in technology, as highlighted in chapter two. A major lesson from history for organizational leaders and managers is to anticipate game changers in their respective industries so as to not be caught off guard and be able to pivot when necessary (e.g., the lessons from Kodak and Sears).

History as Expressions of Gratitude and Honor

As stated in the introduction of this chapter, a sense of history cultivates deeper appreciation and sense of gratitude for accumulated blessings, and honors important individuals and milestones. Suffice it to say that honoring people and milestones and cultivating a sense of appreciation goes a long way toward making people feel valued for their past and future contributions, keeping cherished values in the forefront and endearing internal and external stakeholder for the long haul.

Gratitude is a sentiment that often seems superfluous for people doing their job and out of place in organizational settings driven by self-interest and financial gains. Yet, it is a social glue that generates convivial cooperation and yields a plethora of psychological, social, and organizational benefits (Allen, 2018). Riordan (2013) states in her article, *Foster a Culture of Gratitude*, that employees in organizations where people are valued and appreciated "have high job satisfaction, are willing to work longer hours, engage in productive relationships with co-workers, are motivated to do their best, and work toward achieving the company's goals" (p. 40). She cites a 2012 study from the American Psychological Association that found that "more than half of all employees intended to search for new jobs because they felt underappreciated and undervalued" (p. 4).

A full sense of history reveals that life is unfair, there are winners and losers in the marketplace, and that present-day blessings have come at the expense of those who have gone before. Even a leader's worst day is no worse than the atrocities many others have endured throughout history. Even a leader's best day is attributed to those who have gone before. History at large and organizational histories put present-day struggles and opportunities in context and, for the most part, invite people to count their blessings. History has a unique way to put life into proper perspective.

While there are a variety of small things leaders and managers can do to create cultures of gratitude, taking regular opportunities to share sincere tributes of past and current high-performing employees is a way giving honor to whom honor is due, expose the group to role models, and reinforce organizational values. Rhetorical organizational histories filled with gratitude uniquely conveys to current stakeholders that people matter. When people and important organizational milestones are rightly honored it elevates the expectations for the group. Employee-of-the-month acknowledgments are important but are typically one-time announcements. Hallways with murals that tell the organizational story and are filled with tributes to people can transform wasted wall space and create an ambiance of appreciation and honor.

Conclusion

Learning from experiences is what makes people wiser. Experience is a good teacher when properly evaluated and used to guide growth. History is such a good teacher because it allows mentees to learn from the experiences of others through the evaluated lens of time. As stated earlier, history is a short cut to experience. Knowledge of history at large uniquely fast tracks the development of peoples' emotional, social, and cultural intelligences. It equips leaders and managers to better understand their times and patterns in history to better anticipate probable futures. Rhetorical organizational histories provide competitive advantages and allow leaders and managers keep their cherished values in the forefront of their CAS to endear loyal stakeholders.

This chapter has made a case for organizational leaders and managers to develop a sense of history and think historically to govern their businesses and institutions more wisely. It is fair to say that many leaders and managers who have learned from the past have spared their organizations from various difficulties while those more ignorant of the past could have spared themselves and others from preventable hardships. It would be inconceivable to imagine that organizational leaders would actually go to trial because of their ignorance of history, if it had not actually happened. Leaders can undoubtedly avoid courts of law and infamy by learning from history, but to be on trial for ignorance is a different matter as was the case in the 1919 trial, Henry Ford vs. The Chicago Tribune Company.

Henry Ford sued the Chicago Tribune for one million dollars in damages for calling him an ignorant idealist and anarchist in a June 23, 1916, editorial. The judge in the 1919 trial ruled that "the Tribune was entitled to prove, if it could, that Henry Ford was ignorant" (Butterfield, 1965, p. 55). Ford's words from an earlier interview with Tribune reporter Charles Wheeler, "history is more or less bunk" (Wheeler, 1916), would come back to haunt him. Ford endured a merciless barrage of questions and demonstrated to the court and the newspaper public, much to his chagrin, that he was "quite uneducated" and unable to "rise above the defects of education, at least as to public matters" (Curcio, 2013, p. 111). Reporting on the 1919 trial in the American Bar Journal, Kirkland (1923) noted:

> The charge that Mr. Ford was an ignorant anarchist permitted proof of the plaintiff's knowledge of history, his ability to read, his knowledge of the Revolutionary War, and of his understanding of Benedict Arnold, his understanding that a large army mobilized, his views on the Constitution, etc., etc.
>
> (p. 91)

Although the jury found in Ford's favor and awarded him six cents worth of damages, the spectacle of the trial reinforced his insecurities as an untutored man, hardened his temperament, and pushed him to further isolation.

While driving back from the trial Ford declared that he was "going to build a museum that's going to show industrial history and it won't be bunk" (Liebold, p. 90). The Henry Ford Museum opened with much fanfare ten years later on October 21, 1929, eight days before the Great Depression, forever cementing Ford's conversion to history.

Notes

1. Attributed to Greek historian Thucydides (c. 460 – c. 404 BCE) in the *Art of Rhetoric,* which was falsely attributed to Dionysius (c. 60 – after 7 BCE). – Nadel, G. (1964). Philosophy of History before Historicism. *History and Theory,*

3, 3, 291–315 and Heath, M. (2003). Pseudo-Dionysius Art of Rhetoric 8–11: Figured Speech, Declamation, and Criticism. The *American Journal of Philology*, *124*, 1, 81–105.

2. Francis Bacon (1561–1626), English philosopher, statesman, and essayist observed that, "Histories make men wise; poets witty; mathematics subtile; natural philosophy deep; moral grave; logic and rhetoric able to contend" (Bacon, 1601, The Essays, Of Studies).
3. Reading the room is the ability to capture the silent dialogs as a result of attuned understanding of people in their time and place.
4. This is the spirit and goal of humanities, capture humanity at its best to pass on cherished values and examples that equip people to be at their best.
5. Instead of citing the historical origin and cultural allusion to each term and phrase, readers can "Google" (a term now with its own historical import) them to discover their significance.
6. Happiness referenced in the Declaration of Independence comes from Aristotle's concept of eudemonia, misleadingly translated to happiness. For Aristotle, people are most happy when they are free to pursue what they were uniquely and collective designed for.

References

Allen, S. (2018). *The science of gratitude* [white paper]. Greater Good Science Center at UC Berkley. https://thesnipermind.com/images/Studies-PDF-Format/GGSC-JTF_White_Paper-Gratitude-FINAL.pdf

Almond, J. (1985). *Dictionary of word origins: A history of the words, expressions, and clichés we use.* Citadel Press.

Bandura, A. (1977). *Social learning theory.* Prentice Hall.

Basque, J., & Langley, A. (2018). Invoking alphonse: The founder figure as a historical resource for organizational identity work. *Organizational Studies*, *29*(12), 165–1708.

Besharov, M., & Brickson, S. (2016). Organizational identity and institutional forces. In M. Pratt, M. Schultz, B. Ashforth, & D. Ravasi (Eds.), *The Oxford handbook of organizational identity* (pp. 396–414). Oxford University Press.

Bolman, L., & Deal, T. (2017). *Reframing organizations: Artistry, choice, and leadership* (6th ed.). John Wiley & Sons.

Bourdieu, P. (1986). The forms of capital. In J. Richardson (Ed.), *Handbook of theory and research for the sociology of education* (pp. 241–258). Greenwood Press.

Buckingham, M., & Clifton, D. (2001). *Now, discover your strengths.* The Free Press.

Butterfield, R. (1965). Henry Ford, the Wayside Inn, and the problem of history is bunk. *Proceedings of the Massachusetts Historical Society*, *77*, 53–66.

Cano, E., Moguerza, J., & Redchuk, A. (2012). *Six sigma with R: Statistical engineering for process improvement.* Springer.

Cicero, M. T. (1860). *On oratory and orators* (J.S. Watson, Trans.). Harper & Brothers.

Clark, P., & Rowlinson, Michael. (2004). The treatment of history in organization studies: Toward a "historic turn". *Business History*, *46*(3), 331–352.

Curcio, V. (2013). *Henry Ford.* Oxford University Press.

Devis-Rozental, C. (2018). *Developing socio-emotional intelligence in higher education scholars.* Springer International Publishing.

Foster, W., Suddaby, R., Minkus, A., & Wiebe, E. (2011). History as social memory assets: The example of Tim Hortons. *Management & Organizational History, 6*(1), 101–120.

Gibson, J., & Tesone, D. (2001). Management fads: Emergence, evolution, and implications for managers. *Academy of Management Perspectives, 15*(4), 122–133.

Goleman, D. (1995). *Emotional intelligence.* Bantam Dell.

Goleman, D. (1998). The emotional intelligence of leaders. *Leader to Leader, 1998*(10), 20–26.

Goleman, D. (2006). *Social Intelligence: The new science of human relationships.* Bantam Dell.

Goleman, D., & Boyatzis, R. (2008). Social intelligence and the biology of leadership. *Harvard Business Review, 86*(9), 74.

Hatch, M. J., & Schultz, M. (2002). The dynamics of organizational identity. *Human Relations, 55*(8), 989–1018.

Hayward, S. (2018). *The agile leader: How to create an agile business in the digital age.* Kogan Page Limited.

Iglesias, O., Ind, N., & Schultz, M. (2020). History matters: The role of history in corporate brand strategy. *Business Horizons, Elsevier, 63*(1), 51–60.

Kahn, W., & Fellows, S. (2013). Employee engagement and meaningful work. In B. Dik, Z. Byrne, & M. Steger (Eds.), *Purpose and meaning in the workplace* (pp. 105–126). American Psychological Association.

Kaplan, R., & Norton, D. (1996). *The balanced scoreboard.* Harvard Business Review Press.

Kim, W., & Mauborgne, R. (2004). *Blue ocean strategy: How to create uncontested market space and make the competition irrelevant.* Harvard Business Review Press.

Kirkland, W. (1923). Causes of celebres: IV. Henry Ford vs. The Tribune Company. *American Bar Association Journal, 9*(2), 90–92.

Lasewicz, P. (2015). Forget the past? Or history matters? Selected academic perspectives on the strategic value of organizational pasts. *The American Archivist, 78*(1), 59–83.

Lencioni, P. (2002). *The five dysfunctions of a team.* Jossey-Bass.

Liebold, E. *Reminiscences*, p. 90, Ford Archives, Acc. 65 (Oral History, typed transcripts). Cited in p. Butterfiled, 1965.

McDonald, M. (1996). Strategic marketing planning: Theory, practices, and research agendas. *Journal of Marketing Management, 12*, 4–27.

Mythology. (1833). *Family Magazine*, or *Weekly Abstract of General Knowledge, 1*(15), 122.

Naznin, H. (2013). Correlation between emotional and transformational leadership behavior. *Journal of Business Management, 13*(2), 64–67.

Oertel, S., & Thommes, K. (2018). History as a source of organizational identity creation. *Organization Studies, 39*(12), 1709–1731.

Piazza, A., & Abrahamson, E. (2020). Fads and fashions in management practices: Taking stock and looking Forward. *International Journal of Management Reviews, 22*, 264–286.

Pruitt, Sarah. (2021). 7 things you may not know about MLK's 'I have a dream" speech. *History.com*. www.history.com/news/i-have-a-dream-speech-mlk-facts

Riordan, C. (2013). Foster a culture of gratitude. *Finweek, 40*.

Rowlinson, M. (2013). Management & organizational history: The continuing historic turn. *Management & Organizational History, 8*(4), 327–328.

Santayana, G. (1905). *The life of reason: Introduction and reason in common sense.* The Santayana Edition.

Seaman, J., & Smith, G. (2012). Your company's history as a leadership tool. *Harvard Business Review, 90*(12), 44–52.

Shoup, J., & Hinrichs, T. (2019). *Literature and leadership: The role of the narrative in organizational sensemaking*. Routledge.

Shoup, J., & Studer, S. (2010). *Leveraging chaos: The mysteries of leadership and policy revealed*. Rowman & Littlefield.

Smith, A. (1776). *The wealth of nations*. W. Strahan and T. Cadell.

Smith, G., & Steadman, L. (1981). Present value of corporate history. *Harvard Business Review, 59*(6), 164–173.

St. Croix Collections. (n.d.). Whatever happened to Mr. Knitter? *St. Croix Collections*. www.stcroixcollections.com/whatever-happened-to-mr-knitter/

Suddaby, R., Foster, W., & Trank, C. (2016). Re-membering: Rhetorical history as identity work. In M. Pratt, M. Schultz, B. Ashforth, & D. Ravasi (Eds.). *The Oxford handbook of organizational identity* (pp. 297–316). Oxford University Press.

Vygotsky, L. S. (1978). *Mind in society: The development of higher psychological processes*. Harvard University Press.

Wadhwani, R., Suddaby, R., Mordhorst, M., & Popp, A. (2018). History as organizing: Uses of the past in organization studies. *Organization Studies, 39*(12), 1663–1683.

Wheeler, C. (1916, May 25). *Interview with Henry Ford*. Chicago Tribune.

Zundel, M., Holt, R., & Popp, A. (2016). Using history in the creation of organizational identity. *Management & Organizational History, 11*(2), 211–235.

5 Organizational Histories

Using the Past to Navigate the Future

Introduction

A major premise of this book is that a sense of history prepares leaders and managers to face the future. Connoisseurs of history gain access to experiences that equip them to properly understand and engage humanity in the best and worst of times. As demonstrated in chapter four, history is a mentor that cultivates peoples' emotional, social, and cultural awareness and inspires them to appreciate those responsible for their present-day advantages. Leaders and managers who have a long view of history understand how and why organizations thrive.

Those who judiciously use history are able to invoke larger stories from the past and create meaningful affinities that inspire and endear stakeholders. Many business schools use history to present trends and case studies, but less often how to think historically to gain competitive advantages (Rebeiz, 2011). The principles of this book, and the examples provided below, illustrate how history can be used to shape organizational culture (institutional mindsets and modes of operation), create and maintain brand awareness and competitive advantages, and promote core values. It also provides insight for organizational leaders and managers who are just starting out and do not yet have enough of their own institutional history to leverage. The three companies presented below demonstrate various ways that history contributes to organizational stability and can play a role in corporate strategies.

The Watkins Company – Founded in 1868

It is a rarity for a company to be in existence for over 150 years, let alone be a thriving company, operating in its original community and early buildings. A visit to the Watkins headquarters and facilities located in Winona, Minnesota, a town of approximately 22,000 people on the Mississippi river, evokes a nostalgic and visceral connection between a cherished past and a

DOI: 10.4324/9781003100171-5

desired future. The 1911 modern-classic Watkins Administration building with its mosaic tiled rotunda, 224 stained-glass skylights, and three Tiffany custom stained-glass windows are a testimony to J.R. Watkins' notoriety and his commitment to quality products, which continues to this day. The landmark building, and its historical and architectural significance, are preserved for future Watkins employees and customers as part of the National Register of Historical Places.[1]

Like all companies, The J.R. Watkins Company has humble origins. It started out in a back room of a small house. Unlike many companies, however, it would grow to become a household name in the first half of the 20th century and establish a legacy that remains part of its business model and marketing strategy to this day. In 1868, Joseph Ray Watkins purchased the formula and rights to manufacture and sell Dr. Ward's proven home remedy for sore muscles and aches, common among hardworking farmers and factory workers. J.R. began mass producing the liniment in his home and sold it door-to-door in rural America. Convinced of the quality of his product, J.R. implemented the first money-back guarantee policy with his famous trial line marked bottles. Wary buyers could sample the liniment up to the trial line and get their money back when the Watkins Man returned on his next visit, or if they were pleased with the product they could pay the price for the rest of the bottle.

J.R. relocated his business from Plainview, Minnesota to Winona in 1885, a distance of approximately 26 miles. It was a strategic move as Winona was a major transportation hub supporting three railroads and heavy steamboat traffic. In 1892 Paul Watkins joined his uncle to help run the growing business. In 1895, having established a distribution network, they began manufacturing and selling vanilla extract, black pepper, and cinnamon under the Watkins name and with J.R.'s picture on the labels. By 1910 Watkins products included over 50 items and their salesforce expanded to 2,000 Watkins Men who embodied the Watkins Way. By 1920 the Watkins Company offered 120 items, from spices and extracts to home health and cleaning products. It was the largest direct-selling business in the world.

Watkins' Vanilla Extract, Pepper and Cinnamon were awarded the Gold Medal-Grand Prize for highest quality and biggest value at the 1928 Paris International Exposition. At the 1933 World's Fair in Chicago, Watkins celebrated 65 years of progress and noted in their publicity flier that "There are 9,000 dealers delivering Watkins Products direct from 36 great factories and branches strategically located to give you fresher products and faster service at saving prices" (Watkins Incorporated, 2004, p. 37). The iconic Watkins Men, the pioneer door-to-door independent dealers, created a loyal and growing customer base. The Watkins Man and Way was captured in the 2001 Emmy award-winning movie documentary, *Door to Door*, based upon the inspirational life of Bill Porter, a long time Watkins Man with cerebral palsy who was the top retail salesman in all of Oregon, Idaho, Washington, and California for several years (Watkins Incorporated, 2004, p. 114).

Beginning in 1955, Watkins experienced a yearly decline in sales. The social changes in the 1950s and 1960s, especially the advent of large grocery and retail chain stores, competed against the 15,000 strong Watkins door-to-door salesforce. To woo new customers, Watkins implemented a national advertising campaign with new packaging of its products, celebrity endorsements, television commercials, and ads in *Ebony, Good Housekeeping, McCall's, Reader's Digest,* and the *Saturday Evening Post* (Watkins Incorporated, 2004). With sales still declining, Grace King, the only surviving child of J.R. Watkins, brought in the first non-family president to run the company. The new leadership focused on Watkins' cosmetic line with new colognes and perfumes packaged under new names in hopes of mirroring Avon's success in the market, even though the spices, vanilla, and extracts were the top sellers.

The dwindling Watkins Men and Ladies salesforce and dismal performance in the cosmetic market required Watkins to sell their research farm for agriculture products, overseas assets, and various branch manufacturing facilities to stay solvent. Grace King's grandson was appointed president with the hope that a Watkins heir back at the helm would change the company's financial trajectory. In a second attempt to attract a new generation of customers, Watkins changed its packaging images once again and incorporated more contemporary styles. It also launched a line of gourmet food products under a different name in hopes of generating a new stream of sales, only for it to fail for lack of name recognition.

The changes in leadership to a non-family member president in 1964 and the return to a family member president in 1973 did not yield the intended results. Watkins filed for bankruptcy in 1978. One hundred ten years after J.R. Watkins started his eponymous family business, it would be owned and operated by a different family, the second in its 153-year history. Minneapolis entrepreneur Irwin Jacobs purchased Watkins Products, Inc. and with his son Mark returned Watkins to a profitable company, a turnaround predicated in part on leveraging the company's history. Today Watkins generates over $100 million in sales, has 7,565 direct sales representatives and product placement with major retailers, and lists over 325 products on its website under the domain name of watkins1868.com.

Mark Jacobs, the CEO since 1998 and owner of The Watkins Co. provided one of the authors of this book a tour of the Watkins facility and shared the Watkins' comeback story and his perspectives on why CEOs should think like historians. Mark's atypical route to executive leadership provided him unique vantage points on how to use the past and its stories to lead and manage the company. He earned an undergraduate degree in the liberal arts with a major in French studies from Brown University and was a movie actor and producer prior to joining Watkins in 1996 as vice-president of Sales and Training Development.

Mark noted that history is part of his and Watkins' DNA. The opening page from the modern and iconic looking Watkins 2021 online catalog, *History in the Making* captures this:

Dear Friends,

For 153 years, we have been producing only the finest natural products. All of us at The Watkins Company want to extend our heartfelt thanks for putting your trust in us. Just as our founder J.R. Watkins did when he started this great company in 1868, we strive to give you nothing but the best. Although there have been many changes throughout our long history, what remains a constant are the guiding principles listed below. More than a century ago, our founder called these the "Watkins Way."

We are proud to carry on J.R. Watkins' vision and continue to believe that his way, the Watkins Way, is what makes The Watkins Company and our products so special. Thank you again for being a part of this 153-year-old tradition.

Yours truly,
Mark Jacobs, CEO

The WATKINS WAY

Based on our Founders Principles established over 100 years ago and our goal to be America's most trusted natural products company.

The Highest Quality

We source only the best ingredients worldwide to meet our premium quality standards.

The Best Value

We offer exceptional value for a premium, quality product.

The Neatest Package

We strive to provide a package that is authentic, stylish and convenient for our customers.

The Best Delivery

We aim to exceed our customers' expectations.

The Squarest Terms

We promise to get it right or make it right.

The Fairest Treatment

We treat our customers, our employees and our partners with respect.

The Greatest Uniformity

We provide products that consistently meet our high standards.
The Strictest Integrity We stick consistently with our values.
The Broadest Guarantee

We invented the money-back guarantee in 1868 and continue to stand behind it today.

All of the above Points of Superiority make up
THE WATKINS WAY,
and you will agree that it is a good way.

Mark shared in the interview that when Watkins tried to upscale its image in the 1960s and 1970s, and even in the early 1990s prior to his arrival, it was as if the company was running from its trusted history. Mark shared that when he took over as president, he believed that Watkins should be bragging about its history, marketing its credibility and rich past. He repackaged and rebranded Watkins merchandise with a vintage look, even returning the original liniment trial mark bottle shape used by J.R. Watkins to its classic products, and promoted the use of natural ingredients just as J.R. Watkins did with his liniment, cooking, and bath products. Jacobs used the nostalgic past to connect modern consumers with the trusted Watkins products found in their mothers' and grandmothers' homes.

Mark's father, Irwin Jacobs, is quoted in an October 14, 1997, *Los Angeles Times* article, *A Healthier Future for 'the Watkins Man'* that Mark's business acumen and use of the past was working for Watkins.

"Mark has a passion for what he's doing," he said, adding that his son is the best executive the company has had since emerging from bankruptcy protection.

"Mark has created and promoted a mission statement for the company," Irwin Jacobs said of his son's efforts to link Watkins products with healthy lifestyles. "It is the next generation's view, but none of it extinguishes the past. It promotes the past in going into the future.

(Mills, Karen, October 14, 1997)

Mark shared that he is a steward of Watkins' more than 150-year-old reputation. While Watkins had to modernize, as it did before when it stopped using the horse and buggy to distribute products, that did not mean it had to abandon its history. It needed to use history to stay relevant. As Mark comments, "retro is always hip, just as a nice classic black tuxedo is always in fashion." He acknowledged that Watkins consistently gives a nod to history whenever they can to promote its values and make favorable associations with their products, especially for those with positive childhood memories growing up with Watkins' products at their kitchen and picnic tables. Mark noted that for Watkins, history is everything – it established trust early on with its customers and went on to link generations with timeless quality organic products, even providing a sense of comfort during three centuries of world changes including the Great Depression, WWI, and WWII.

That Watkins takes it celebrated history seriously is not only evident in its iconic packaging and marketing strategies and tactics, but also in that it has its own archivist and houses its own museum next to its historical 1911 monumental administration building. The Watkins Museum opened in 1993 and resides on the first floor of the company's former printing plant that was responsible for producing millions of copies of their famous Watkins almanacs, cookbooks, catalogs, and product labels.

John Goplen, Watkins' archivist, shared that the museum had 10,000 to 15,000 tourists every year, prior to the COVID pandemic. He reported that the impetus for launching a museum involved several considerations – the upcoming 125th anniversary, it was a good marketing opportunity, provided a special place for visitors from the many riverboat and bus tours making their way through Winona, and the physical space becoming available when the printing plant closed after 88 years in operation.

When asked why Watkins needed a full-time archivist, John reported that there was so much wasted history scattered about that could be used to help with marketing and research. When asked why organizational histories matter, John shared that history provides personal connections between the present and the past and that nostalgia "has a way of flooding memories." In this case, Watkins' nostalgia connects to many customers' childhood memories and brings those memories to the forefront of the mind. John noted that today people are bombarded with advertisements lacking personal connection. In contrast, Watkins uses its memorable and iconic past to make both meaningful and relevant connections with its existing and new consumers.

The Watkins history is also memorialized with pictures and text in the *Images of America* series published by Arcadia Publishing. The book *Watkins Incorporated* reached a conclusion that echoes the theme of this book – "The future of Watkins can be found in the past. The traditions of quality products and customer service that began with J.R. Watkins in 1868 continue today and will be just as recognizable 100 years from now" (Watkins Incorporated, 2004, p. 128).

Mark acknowledged not only being a fan of Watkins' history, but history in general, noting that "history teaches everything." He mentioned that business executives need to wear at least two hats – the entrepreneur who has a "magical vision" and the CEO who understands that history is "all that we really have" when trying to discern what will work and not work. Mark also commented that a sense of history provides important understandings of human nature and how to prudently deal with human beings at their best, worst, and anywhere in between. In addition, he noted a couple of times in the conversation that a sense of history has a way of keeping people humbled, emphasizing that leaders really need humility.

The Watkins story illustrates how organizational histories can be strategically and tactically leveraged to regain a competitive edge, similar to the comeback story of Adidas outlined in chapter four. For companies just starting out, leaders and managers can borrow other histories in the interim, until their own histories are established. For example, Starbucks began in the seaport community of Seattle and took its name from a character in *Moby Dick* to tap into "the romance of the high seas and the seafaring tradition of the early coffee traders" (Starbucks, n.d.). The luxury Montblanc brand started in Hamburg Germany 1908 as the Simplo Filler Pen Company pen only later in 1910 to release a pen with the French name for the highest mountain in the Alps, the peak of Europe, Mont Blanc. The new name branded their product with the grandeur of the perpetual White (Blanc) Mountain (Mont) and the chic elegance associated with France.

Edwards Lifesciences – Founded 1958; Publicly Incorporated 2000

The corporate headquarters of Edwards Lifesciences stands in contrast to the historical buildings at the center of the Watkins Company. The Irvine, California campus reflects the substantial growth of the business since it spun off from Baxter International as a publicly traded company in 2000. It is the headquarters of a global corporation of more than 16,000 employees.[2] The contemporary architectural design includes open floorplans, large windows, and ample outdoor meeting spaces to create an environment of creativity and connectivity. It reflects a company focused on innovation and collaboration, dedicated to providing better solutions to patients suffering from heart disease.[3]

The company's history is also deeply evident throughout the campus. The buildings and walkways are filled with the stories of innovators and patients who have impacted, and been impacted by, the company's journey. The main interior walkway leading to the conference center includes panels outlining the company's 60+ year history of innovation and patient care. Opposite these panels are pictures that honor the legacy partners who joined with the company over the years to develop the lifesaving technology at the heart of the business. The main atrium is dedicated to Dr. Albert Starr, co-founder of the company and partner to Miles "Lowell" Edwards, creators of the first commercially successful artificial heart valve. The headquarters includes a museum dedicated to the development and evolution of the heart valve and the critical care devices that sustain hospital patients. These highlight the company's purpose and identity: "Helping patients is our life's work, and life is now."

Edwards Lifesciences traces its roots to 1958, when Lowell Edwards approached the young doctor Albert Starr at the University of Oregon Medical School with an ambitious plan to develop an artificial heart. He was motivated, in part, by his own health, as he had developed heart disease due to scarring in his heart valves from a bout rheumatic fever as a teenager. Edwards himself was a retired mechanical engineer specializing in hydraulics. He had developed the centrifugal spinning pump that Boeing used for the B-17 bomber during WWII that enabled it to fly at high altitudes. He reasoned that the heart was a sophisticated hydraulic pump that could be imitated through mechanical engineering. Starr convinced him to focus his research on developing a heart valve instead, since no one had developed any of the components necessary for an artificial heart and there was great need among Dr. Starr's patients for a replacement heart valve. Within two years they had built and successfully placed in a patient the world's first artificial heart valve: the Starr-Edwards mitral valve.[4] This achievement led to the creation of Edwards Laboratories in Santa Ana, California in April 1961.

Edwards Laboratories was an innovative company that typified the medical industry in the 1950s and 1960s. Its focus on heart care and collaborative relationships with doctors is the foundation for the company's current identity and purpose. By the late 1960s Edwards Laboratories had partnered with most of the regional hospitals in southern California. Some of the company's earliest employees would also go on to establish other medical device companies specializing in heart care. Shiley Laboratories, Bently Laboratories, and Hancock Laboratories each began as an outgrowth of their founders' work at Edwards.

Lowell Edward's decision to sell his business to the Chicago-based American Hospital Supply Corporation in 1966 also expanded the company's national market. The company was renamed American Edwards Laboratories to reflect its role as part of American Hospital Supply, though the parent organization's decentralized model of leadership allowed Edwards to maintain an independent identity. Edwards Laboratories continued to direct its own research and development in collaboration with partners from the medical community. American Hospital Supply became the exclusive distributor of Edwards medical devices.

This collaborative environment pushed Edwards to extend its brand to new areas of patient care. The stories behind these developments are an important part of corporate identity and serve to inspire ongoing innovation. The Fogarty balloon catheter was the company's second major technological breakthrough and represents one of the most important cardio-vascular innovations of the era. Dr. Thomas Fogarty had conceived of this device to safely remove arterial blood clots while a student at the University of Cincinnati's medical school. Albert Starr, who had become his supervisor at the University of Oregon in 1965, put him in contact with his longtime friend Lowell Edwards to help arrange its engineering. Fogarty received a patent for the device in 1969 and assigned Edwards Laboratories the right to manufacture the product. It became the first non-invasive procedure to treat thrombosis, substantially increasing the survival rate of patients suffering from blood clots.

The Fogarty catheter became the springboard for the third major medical device produced by Edward Laboratories: the Swan-Ganz catheter. This device grew out of the company's relationship with Dr. Jeremy Swan, chief of cardiology at Cedars-Sinai Medical Center in Los Angeles, who served as a consultant for Edwards' catheter-based projects in the late 1960s. The hospital was an early innovator in critical care, and he sought to find better ways to monitor patients who suffered from myocardial infarction. His solution was to combine a pulmonary-artery catheter first used in 1967 by Dr. Ronald Bradley in London with the Fogarty balloon as a flotation guide to bring the catheter to the heart by way of the jugular artery. Edwards Laboratories produced prototypes of the device in 1969, and Dr. Swan partnered with Dr. William Ganz to test the concept. Swan and Ganz were able to patent the device in 1970, using Edwards Laboratories as its manufacturer.

The artificial heart valve, Fogarty balloon catheter, and Swan-Ganz catheter anchored research and development at Edwards Laboratories during the 1970s. The company employed more than 1600 people by the early-1980s and was organized around three primary business units: cardiovascular, noninvasive procedures, and critical care. Ongoing collaboration with doctors and surgeons significantly expanded the use of the Swan-Ganz catheter with the addition of new diagnostic equipment that could connect with the device.[5] Edwards also transitioned to the use of bioprosthetic heart valves. The company partnered with Dr. Alain Carpentier in 1975, a pioneer of reconstructive valve surgery, to develop a long-lasting porcine valve for patients suffering from aortic stenosis. This partnership continued for decades as they developed new generations of the porcine valve.

In 1986 American Hospital Supply Corporation merged with Baxter International Inc., which absorbed Edwards Laboratories and transformed it into their new CardioVascular division. Although the division continued to develop Edward's core technologies, it was now responsible for all aspects of cardiovascular care. For example, the division partnered with Dr. Delos "Toby" Cosgrove to develop an annuloplasty system to correct functional tricuspid regurgitation in the mitral valve, which is located between the left atrium and left ventricle of the heart. However, this type of development was in competition with other priorities. This included the addition of blood-filtration devices and heart-lung bypass machines used during open-heart surgery. In 1996, Baxter also announced that the division would be partnering with its Biotech Group to develop a product to control bleeding during surgery.[6]

Baxter International provided an international market for the Edwards brand. At the same time, the CardioVascular Group was the poorest performing division in profitability throughout the 1990s, despite a continued commitment to add new acquisitions to its product line. Mike Mussallem, who served as Vice-President of CardioVascular at the time, believes that the division's low performance was based on its wide diversity of interests: "we became part of a much larger company, and we just lost this way [of innovation]."[7] He became part of a strategy to spin off the business unit as an independent company focusing exclusively on structural heart disease and critical care.

Edwards Lifesciences became a publicly held company on the New York Stock Exchange on April 3, 2000. Mike Mussallem, who transitioned from Baxter to become the company's first CEO, graciously provided one of this book's authors with an interview on the company's priorities and the role of history in shaping Edwards' general direction and identity (Mussallem, 2021). As a company built on technological innovation, he emphasizes that corporate strategy always looks towards the future. Yet the company's priorities are built around the original ideals exhibited by the partnership of Lowell Edwards and Albert Starr, whose goals were to create technology that could offer better solutions to patients suffering from cardio-vascular disease. These priorities are captured well in the current company's Credo:

> At Edwards Lifesciences, we are dedicated to providing innovative solutions for people fighting cardiovascular disease.
>
> Through our actions, we will become trusted partners with customers, colleagues, and patients – creating a community unified in its mission to improve the quality of life around the world. Our results will benefit customers, patients, employees, and shareholders.
>
> We will celebrate our successes, thrive on discovery, and continually expand our boundaries. We will act boldly, decisively, and with determination on behalf of people fighting cardiovascular disease.
>
> Helping patients is our life's work, and *life is now.*

Mike Mussallem first encountered Edwards in 1988 when he took a role within Baxter's CardioVascular division. His pathway to leadership in the field of medical technology was unconventional. He worked his way through college in a steel mill to earn a degree in chemical engineering. He quickly discovered upon graduation that the most common jobs for chemical engineers were less than fulfilling to him. After working on anti-freeze at Union Carbide, he joined Baxter International as part of their manufacturing team in 1979. He describes Baxter as a business that emphasized meritocracy, which gave him a wide array of experiences that enabled him to progress from manufacturing to general management. It eventually led to his promotion to lead the CardioVascular Group in 1994.

Mike shared that his experience as Vice President of the least performing sector at Baxter had a big impact on how he feels about history. He became a student of innovation and knew that the division needed to take a different path for the future. He needed to learn "why and how companies innovate." More particularly he turned his attention toward the history of Edwards, its previous success, and its shortcomings. As Mike put it: "What was the history of Edwards? Why did it stop? What do we have to do to get it going again?" His investigation highlighted the central role of innovation in the field of cardiovascular technology as key to the organization's early success. History became a guide as he organized Edwards Lifesciences to capture the original spirit of the company.

The stories of Lowell Edwards and Albert Starr continue to provide the foundation for the organization's identity and purpose. Lowell's commitment to the impact of technology on heart disease became "a driving force . . . this idea that you can transform the treatment of the patient . . . and that you can have an impact on that, just elevates and makes all of our, not only careers, but all of our lives more important." Mike emphasizes Lowell's curiosity and boldness in adapting his skills in hydraulic engineering to pursue the creation of an artificial heart, even if he ended up with a heart valve instead. Lowell's story also demonstrates the human side of medical technology; he wrestled with his own personal struggle with heart disease and sought to help others who were suffering from the same illness. His example illustrates the company's 'secret sauce' of principles: focus on patient needs, big dreams, and willingness to fail and learn from mistakes.

Mike points to Edwards Lifesciences' long history of innovation as an inspiration toward future projects. He continues to leverage the company's original strengths in heart valves and catheter technology as a basis for organizational development. "We ultimately landed on the idea of focusing on structural heart disease and critical care where we are today, which we think is a more impactful way for us to do our work." He notes that this type of specialization is the opposite way many med-tech companies operate.

Their most recent line of heart valves, transcatheter aortic valve replacement (TAVR), integrates both strengths to provide a non-invasive alternative to valve repair in seriously ill patients. This technology represents the company's commitment to the concept of disruption – innovation that seeks to replace pre-existing technology with something better. This idea is not new. The porcine valve produced in the 1970s represents this same shift in technology, effectively replacing the original line of mechanical heart valves first developed by Edwards and Starr. Since 2017, TAVR has become a more prominent alternative to surgery in patients beyond the most critically ill.

Ultimately Mike views the organization's history as central to its corporate identity. This was an important lesson from early in his tenure as CEO. Initially, he was committed to developing a modern synthesized name that matched the trends of the Dot-com era. Market research pointed him in a slightly different direction. "Every time we did a survey, our employees and customers voted for the Edwards name above our created names. And after 2, 3, 4 of these surveys we got the message." He modernized the company name by substituting "Lifesciences" for "Laboratories," but honored the stakeholders' interests by preserving "Edwards."

Corporate history plays an important role in shaping the Edwards community. The main campus in Irvine is filled with images and displays aimed at connecting the past and the present to build toward future goals. These create a connection between employees, medical partners, and patients. Mike points to the early years of the company's history as a model of compassion and resiliency. History matters because it offers "compassion for what our early innovators probably worked through and lived through," giving "a sense of resilience the next time we face challenges." It also emphasizes the importance of clinical partnerships as an ongoing priority for the company. This was a centerpiece of the company's 60th-anniversary celebration in 2018. The main dinner featured many of the prominent engineers and partners who contributed to the core technologies responsible for the company's success. More importantly, the celebration highlighted their significance in improving patient care for those suffering from heart disease.

Edwards is a unique example of a corporation that has witnessed dramatic change in a relatively short time span in both organizational structure and independence. It points to the way history can be used as the starting point for new directions while maintaining a core commitment to an organization's original ideals. Their dedication to the innovative environment of the company's early years is matched by their ongoing effort to create historical imprints that reflect its 20-year history as a publicly traded company. Corporate identity represents past innovators and the patients who receive treatment with medical devices produced by current employees. These are highlighted in corporate videos about patients who received valve replacements or other care through devices created at Edwards. They are shown in all global offices and manufacturing plants to showcase the personal value of the company's work. The ongoing history of collaborative innovation and patient care literally covers the walls of the corporate headquarters. Mike Mussallem's hope for the future of the company is that it will continue to embrace a culture of putting patients first, and that it will continue to pursue innovations that will replace current practices with something better.

The Walt Disney Company – Founded 1923

It is difficult to find someone who has never heard of The Walt Disney Company. What started as a small animation studio is now one of the largest multi-media and entertainment companies in the world. The corporate headquarters in Burbank, California still houses the buildings Walt Disney constructed from the profits he made off *Snow White and the Seven Dwarfs* (1937), his first feature length animated film. Walt's office in suite 3H of the old animation studio was restored in 2016 to showcase part of the company's history. Corporate leadership occupies the newer 'Team Disney – The Michael D. Eisner Building' near the main entrance. Column statues of the seven dwarfs symbolically hold up the roof in homage to the film that financed the move to Burbank in 1939.[8]

Walt Disney and his characters have served as the heart of the Walt Disney Company for more than 95 years. The *Partners* statue of Walt and Mickey stands in four of the company's theme parks: Disneyland, the Magic Kingdom at Walt Disney World, Walt Disney Studios Park near Paris, and Tokyo Disney. A parallel *Storytellers* statue of a young Walt leaning on a suitcase topped with Mickey Mouse appears in Disney California Adventure, Tokyo DisneySea, and Shanghai Disneyland. These monuments honor the business' origin and connect each theme park by common inspiration. Both statues speak to the dreams and ambition that have defined the company since its inception in 1923. They highlight the ongoing integration of media entertainment, technology, and themed experiences that characterized Walt's business development.

The Walt Disney Company has humble roots. It was founded on October 16, 1923, to fulfill a contract to produce a series of short films about a girl trapped in a cartoon world. Walt and his brother Roy moved to Hollywood from Kansas City, Missouri after their first company, Laugh-O-Gram Studios, went bankrupt. They established The Disney Brothers Studio after selling the distribution rights to *Alice's Wonderland*, changing the company name to Walt Disney Studios in 1926 when they moved to a new location in Los Angeles. The studio on Hyperion Avenue allowed the brothers to gain control of their intellectual property and establish financial independence. Walt created Mickey Mouse after realizing that he had signed away control of his first major cartoon character, Oswald the Lucky Rabbit. Mickey appeared in *Steamboat Willie* in 1928, the first animated film to synchronize animation with sound. This innovation enabled the company to sign distribution rights directly with major studios instead of working through an agent.

The financial challenges of the Great Depression set the framework for the company's future success. Major studios were willing to partner with Disney but were unwilling to advance any money to help with production costs. The Disney brothers responded by reorganizing the business as Walt Disney Productions and creating three subsidiary companies. Walt Disney Enterprises handled the licensing of Disney characters, the Liled Realty and Investment Company managed real estate, and the Disney Film Recording Company allowed the studio to produce its own sound and music. Merchandizing brought in hundreds of thousands of dollars each year to subsidize their films. These resources allowed Walt to expand his workforce and embark on the production of *Snow White and the Seven Dwarfs*.

The move to Burbank in 1939 signified Disney's transition from a smaller corporation to a larger business. Full-length animated films became the priority. This elevated the role of the "Nine Old Men," as Walt dubbed them in the 1950s, to become the primary guardians of his filmmaking vision. Roy convinced his brother to take the company public on the New York Stock Exchange to add investors to help pay for the expanded production costs. However, government contracts during World War II used most of the workforce toward the production of wartime propaganda and training videos. This led to a period of adaptation that ultimately expanded the studio's film offerings. By 1950 Disney was producing live-action films and nature documentaries in addition to its animated features.[9] Disney also created its own distribution arm, Buena Vista Film Distribution, ending the company's dependence on other organizations to release its films.

The company's investment in television programs was tied directly to Walt's passion project – Disneyland.[10] Walt started this project in 1951 when he registered Disneyland, Inc. as a joint venture corporation. He founded WED Enterprises with his own money in 1952 to design the amusement park and its attractions. Roy searched for investors after the project received approval from Disney's board of directors. They reached an agreement with ABC in March 1954 that guaranteed financing in return for a weekly television program and a share of park revenues. The *Disneyland* show was the first of Disney's successive anthology programs. This allowed Walt to promote his park while associating its themed lands with his movie characters. Disneyland opened its doors on July 17, 1955, to an audience of more than

90 million people on live television. This integration of media entertainment and interactive experiences has remained Walt Disney Company's primary business.

Disneyland is a tangible expression of Walt's creative vision. It was the first "theme park," allowing guests to immerse themselves in lands that reflected the various films produced by the movie studio. It was also designed to celebrate human achievement, a place where the past meets the future. Guests pass through a gateway underneath an elevated train station into Main Street U.S.A., a representation of Disney's hometown of Marceline, Missouri. This street leads to a round-about that connects to four themed lands. On the left are gateways to Adventureland and Frontierland, which celebrate the natural world and the spirit of exploration. Sleeping Beauty's castle lies straight ahead, the entrance into Fantasyland, which transports guests into a land inspired by Disney's animated films. The entrance to Tomorrowland is on the right. This was originally designed to be an evolving display of what is possible through human innovation. Today it is largely dedicated to attractions themed around outer space.

Walt always considered the park to be a work in progress, a playground that he would constantly improve through innovation. This was no different than his approach to film production. He was the first to implement new technologies to his animated films: synchronized sound, Technicolor, the multiplane camera, and surround sound. The imaginative engineers at WED Enterprises, known as Imagineers, developed a type of robotic animation called Animatronics that revolutionized immersive attractions. The Tiki Room, which opened in 1963, used this technology to synchronize sounds to robotic birds. This enabled Walt to receive corporate sponsorships to produce attractions for the 1964 World's Fair in New York, where he revealed the proto-type Audio-Animatronic of Abraham Lincoln and the more expansive Carousel of Progress, a rotating stage show that celebrates technological advancement throughout the 20th century. Walt used the profits from his film Mary Poppins to create MAPO, a division responsible for building Audio-Animatronic technology for themed rides.

Walt Disney's death in 1966 created a void in the company's creative leadership. The next five years saw his brother Roy complete a variety of projects that were already in various stages of development. Walt Disney World near Orlando, Florida was the landmark achievement of his tenure as CEO. The corporate leadership team struggled to agree on a path forward after Roy's death in 1971. Richard Sherman, a longtime collaborator who wrote music for Disney films and attractions, later comments that "we had a board of directors that was not quite sure where they were going. They were always trying to say 'what would Walt do' instead of what would 'we' do."[11] The goal became to create films and build attractions that would appeal to a teenage audience. The theme parks fared better than the movie studio. The development of Space Mountain (1971) and Big Thunder Mountain Railroad (1979) successfully adapted rollercoasters to the immersive nature of Disney attractions. A reimagined version of EPCOT, dedicated to the exploration of technology, the natural world, and global cultures opened at Walt Disney World in 1982. By then most of the company's revenue came from its theme parks division.

The company entered a new age of growth and vitality after surviving an attempt at a hostile takeover in 1984. The board of directors sought leadership from outside the company, hiring Michael Eisner as CEO and Frank Wells as President of the organization. As a team they revitalized the company, investing heavily in theme parks and leading a revival of its film division. They transformed Disney into a global multi-media corporation, now The Walt Disney Company, reorganizing and rebranding its various divisions. They leveraged new technology in the television industry to expand their media presence, entering the home video market and moving the Disney brand to cable TV. Eisner himself became the face of the company's media presence, hosting the *Wonderful World of Disney* on Sunday nights in the same manner that Walt hosted his television shows.

Michael Eisner presided over two very different eras for The Walt Disney Company. He was responsible for Disney's revival by the late 1980s and some of its struggles at the turn of the century. Like many corporate leaders at that time, he relied on breadth to sustain growth. Corporate partnerships added greater depth to the company's ventures. Some of the best attractions were produced alongside Lucasfilm and MGM, the latter allowing Eisner to use their films for the development of Disney-MGM Studios at Walt Disney World. In 1990 Eisner announced "The Disney Decade," an expansion plan that included hotels, rides, and new theme parks. This extended beyond Disney's core business to include the creation of a radio station and cruise line, along with the acquisition of the ABC television network and two sports teams in Anaheim. Euro-Disney near Paris was to be his crowning achievement. Eddie Sotto, former Senior Vice President of Concept Design, remarks that Eisner "wasn't just a typical CEO executive. He wanted to be part of the creative process, and Disneyland Paris was the mark they were to make." Eisner wanted to distinguish himself from Walt and Roy by creating the most beautiful park, inspired by European culture and French design.

The transition from Michael Eisner to Bob Iger in 2005 was similar to the change in leadership two decades before. By 2000 the theme parks division was the only part of the company performing well. This went into decline after the terrorist attacks in 2001 and was exacerbated by the poor reception to Disney's California Adventure in Anaheim when it opened the following year. Eisner had become more conservative in his investments after Euro-Disney struggled financially and new programs on ABC received poor ratings. The lackluster quality of the new theme park offered a visible imprint of his new strategy. Bob Iger put the problem this way: "I think the biggest damage was the mindset that there was a new formula. Let's build a park for half the budget, let's deliver half the product, and let's ignore all these wonderful things Walt had created."

The Bob Iger era at the Walt Disney Company was one of unprecedented prosperity, built on Walt Disney's legacy and the original business model set in place by Michael Eisner. Iger had been President of the ABC network during its acquisition by Disney in 1996. Eisner brought him into executive leadership at the Walt Disney Company, first as President of Disney International in 1999, and then as President and COO of the company in 2000. He spent 15 years as CEO, handing the reigns to Bob Chapek in March 2020 when he transitioned to the role of Executive Chairman. Although he retired in December 2021, the company still represents his influence. Much of what follows comes from Iger's book *The Ride of a Lifetime* (2019) and public comments about his approach to the company, its heritage, and the future. Bob Iger gave a series of interviews about his time as CEO during his last year an a half with the company. See Faber (2021), Parker (2021), Rubenstein (2020), and Schwartzel & Fritz (2020).

The Walt Disney Company continues to operate under the mission statement first established by Walt Disney in 1955:

> The mission of The Walt Disney Company is to entertain, inform and inspire people around the globe through the power of unparalleled storytelling, reflecting the iconic brands, creative minds and innovative technologies that make ours the world's premier entertainment company.[12]

Iger will be remembered for high-profile acquisitions that have greatly enhanced Disney's intellectual property: Pixar, Marvel, Lucasfilm, and 20th Century Fox. Yet before he turned his attention to further expansion, he focused on safeguarding Walt Disney's core business – its animation studio. Iger understood that The Walt Disney Company's diverse properties were held together by the characters created for its media entertainment. He writes that "Disney Animation *was* the brand. It was the fuel that powered many of our other businesses, including consumer products, television, and theme parks" (Iger, 2019, p. 133). The decision to acquire Pixar was motivated, in part, to use their creative leads to help revitalize Disney's animation studio. He reiterated this point in a recent interview with NBC's David Faber: "You look at 'Frozen' and you look at 'Moana' . . . and the number of Academy Awards and the box-office success . . . everything that we've done at Disney animation since then was tied to the Pixar acquisition" (Parker, 2021).

The interrelationship between media entertainment and theme parks was the centerpiece of Disney's business model under Iger's stewardship and remained consistent with Walt's original vision. He considers the development of Shanghai Disney as the crowning achievement of his career (Iger, 2019, p. ix). It fulfilled all three of his key strategies for corporate success: high-quality branded content, technological innovation, and global orientation. Yet his initial foray into theme park design was to improve California Adventure. He accomplished this by blending the past and future, leaning heavily on Walt Disney's early history as a filmmaker while establishing the park as the home to Pixar's animated characters. The Imagineers completely redesigned the entrance to represent Walt's arrival in Hollywood. This included the first *Storytellers* statue, located across from a recreation of the Cathay Circle Theater, signifying the start of a new life. This transformed the park into a celebration of Walt's creative vision and its legacy into the 21st century.

One of the biggest creative challenges for the company is managing change when the business thrives on a sense of nostalgia. Iger views Disney's history as an asset that can be leveraged alongside innovation, though he also believes that the company needs to be committed to progress. He comments:

> [Disney's] heritage is still the way, is still inviting, is still entertaining. There's no need to discard it and no need to be disdainful of it. There is also no need to be reverential to it, because if you revere something and you don't want anything to change, you might as well relegate it to a museum case.

The most recognizable blend of Disney heritage and innovation can be seen in the Disney parks. During Iger's tenure some attractions received upgrades or other changes when they went down for refurbishment. In 2009, It's a Small World reopened at Disneyland with a new 'Spirit of America' room and the addition of 29 characters from Disney and Pixar movies. Pirates of the Caribbean has received a series of changes over the years. The first came in the 1990s when a scene was modified to reflect hungry pirates chasing after food rather than women. The storyline received an overhaul in 2006 to connect the ride to the blockbuster movie *Pirates of the Caribbean: The Curse of the Black Pearl*. This included new Audio-Animatronics representing characters from the film. More recent changes reflect Iger's belief that the company needs to reflect changing standards of behavior. The auction scene in Pirates of the Caribbean now represents the sale of stolen goods rather than a bridal auction.

Iger understands that he has been the guardian of Walt Disney's legacy. He believes this goes beyond preserving the Disney brand. Speaking at the opening ceremony for Walt Disney World's 50th Anniversary, he reminded the crowd that one of Walt's lasting legacies is "the responsibility we have as storytellers, to continuously reinvent the way that we all tell stories, and to use technology to immerse guests deeper into the story world that they love so much" (2021, October 1). This legacy shaped the way Iger incorporated new brands into the Walt Disney Company. He focused on entertainment companies whose characters and stories could easily fit within Disney's culture. Some of the most immersive attractions at the Disney parks today are based on stories produced by Lucasfilm and Marvel studios, the two companies that were on the top of Iger's list after incorporating Pixar. Each have received their own "lands" in Disney parks, with attractions that bring park guests into the story.[13]

The 18-month celebration of Walt Disney World's 50th Anniversary (2021–2022) is just the latest in a long tradition of honoring important milestones in the company's history. Each year the company celebrates the "birthday" of its original cartoon characters with special desserts at its theme parks. Attractions also receive special attention. Disneyland sold tickets to a midnight celebration for the 50th Anniversary of the Haunted Mansion on August 8–9, 2019. The waiting area for Great Moments with Mr. Lincoln on Main Street was converted to display artifacts from the Walt Disney Archives and tell the story of the ride's development during the 1960s and later additions to "plus" attraction. This presentation was transformed into a documentary that is part of the Disney+ series *Behind the Attraction* (2021). These episodes showcase not only the development of important attractions in Disney history but also their evolution and influence on later themed experiences.

The Walt Disney Company is driven by memory and imagination. Bob Chapek, the company's new CEO, recalled his own early trips to Walt Disney World when giving his opening address for the park's 50th-anniversary celebration. He comments that "Walt's biggest dream was to create a fully immersive place unlike anywhere else, where characters and stories could come to life to entertain and delight guests of all ages" (2021, October 1). Disney's dream became a six-part documentary series *The Imagineering Story* (Iwerks, 2019) on Disney+, highlighting the creative talent behind the innovations that shaped Disney theme parks. Archival film footage and live interviews from Disney Imagineers and corporate executives trace the role of Disney Imagineering from its inception to the development of Shanghai Disney. It places future projects in a trajectory started by Walt Disney and the people who first helped built the company.

The past meets the present each day at the corporate headquarters in Burbank, California. The buildings are named after important contributors to the company's history. The Legends Plaza in front of the "Team Disney" building honors the animators, actors, songwriters, business leaders and other employees who have made a significant impact on the company's growth. A colonnade includes copper plaques representing people who have received the Disney Legends Award. At its entrance stands one of the *Partners* statues of Walt and Mickey. To the side sits a statue of his brother Roy seated on a park bench next to Minnie Mouse. The names of some of these recipients appear in the window along Main Street in Disney's theme parks around the globe. The Walt Disney Company reminds employees and guests alike that it is built on legends, and that the past is an inspiration to the future.

Conclusion

The Watkins Company, Edwards Lifesciences, and The Walt Disney Company are dedicated to very different goals, but there are some important similarities in their histories. Each company began as a small business under the personal guidance of its founder. Over time they faced periods of decline or stagnation as they experienced new competition in their industries, adapting to a changing marketplace by leveraging new technologies to improve their products and reach new customers. At various points, they responded by diversifying their offerings beyond the core mission that had defined them. Revitalization came by recentering on their core values and expanding under a more nuanced approach to diversification.

Mark Jacobs, Mike Mussallem, and Bob Iger represent ways that business leaders should leverage the past to strengthen their companies. Their views of history align with the main principles introduced in chapter four. History informs the core values and key goals that shape their business strategies, offering a sense of purpose that has guided their ambitions. Each learned that corporate history was already part of their respective company's DNA. Understanding and using this history enables them to connect with their employees and customers. History defines the symbols that evoke a sense of nostalgia and stir personal memories about their companies and their brands. It connects current and future objectives with endearing legacies, binding new products and services to past practices while also justifying new directions. Moreover, a sense of history enables them to emphasize the human relationships and hard work at the heart of their organizations.

Every company has a past that can be meaningful to each business leader when evaluated from a historical mindset. Those with a cultivated sense of history are positioned to engage in parallel thinking when pursuing a vision and rendering consequential decisions. This way of thinking searches for universal and emerging patterns on ways the social world worked in the past (the meta-narrative) in relation to the present (the current narrative). Leaders who think this way can expand their observations to make comparable adaptive changes that are most likely to bring success around core values and functions that extend from the past to a desired future. They are also able to identify potential trajectories, good and bad, through a contextual comparison of past events and emerging trends.

Notes

1. Unless otherwise designated, the documented history of The Watkins Co. cited in this section are from various exhibits in the Watkins Museum located at 150 Liberty Street, Winona, MN.
2. Edwards had an employee count of 16, 105 as of October 2021.
3. The following represents a synthesis from resources provided by Edwards Lifesciences or published in medical journals. See Edwards Lifesciences (2020), Edwards Lifesciences (2021), Fogarty Innovation (2013), Herper (2019), Hilal & Erikson (1981), Matthews (1998).
4. The advent of the Starr-Edwards mechanical valve marked the beginning of the modern era for heart valve replacement.
5. The Swan-Ganz Artery Catheter is equipped to measure advanced hemodynamic parameters. It measures cardiac output, mixed venous oxygen saturation, stroke volume, systemic vascular resistance, right ventricular ejection fracture, right ventricular end diastolic volume, right atrial pressure, pulmonary artery pressure, and pulmonary artery occlusion pressure. See Chatterjee (2009).
6. Baxter International 1996 Annual Report.
7. All quotes come from an interview conducted on August 3, 2021, with Mike Mussallem, CEO of Edwards Lifesciences.
8. The Walt Disney Company provides an overview of their company's history at www.d23.com/disney-history. (Disney History) It also forms the central narrative in documentary series *The Imagineering story* (Iwerks, 2019). Details on Walt Disney's personal life and business perspective comes from Gabler (2007).
9. Walt Disney produced a series of nature documentaries under the series *True-Life Adventures* beginning in 1948. The studio marked its return to animated features in 1950 with the release of *Cinderella*. Disney's first live-action film, *Treasure Island*, was also released that year.
10. Disney's first television special, *An Hour in Wonderland*, aired on December 25, 1950 in partnership with The Coca-Cola Company.
11. Unless otherwise noted, all quotes come from the documentary series *The Imagineering Story* (Iwerks, 2019).
12. Disney's mission statement is feature prominently in its corporate website: https://thewaltdisneycompany.com/about/.
13. For example, Disney designed an immersive land for the Star Wars franchise, creating the fictional planet of Baatu at Disneyland and Disney's Hollywood Studios at Walt Disney World. Cast members act as residents of Black Spire Outpost. Guests can become smugglers working for Hondo Ohnaka, taking various roles in the cockpit of the iconic Millennium Falcon on Millennium Falcon: Smuggler's Run. They can become members of the Resistance fleeing the First Order in the multi-stage attraction Rise of the Resistance, which takes them through a queue that proceeds from the Resistance base, a flight simulator, and the halls of a Star Destroyer before boarding a trackless ride vehicle that moves them through the remainder of the starship and then back to the planet of Batuu.

References

Chatterjee, K. (2009). The Swan-Ganz catheters: Past, present, and future. *Circulation, 119*, 47–152.

Disney History. *Walt Disney archives*. https://d23.com/disney-history/

Edwards Lifesciences. (2020, September 18). Welcome to Edwards lifesciences [Video]. *YouTube*. www.youtube.com/watch?v=x6qceIH5vD4

Edwards Lifesciences. (2021, October 15). *Edwards celebrates 60 years of discovery* [Video]. *YouTube*. www.youtube.com/watch?v=Tj4QWI95ER4

Faber, D. (2021, December 21). *Interview with Bob Iger* [Video]. *CNBC*. www.cnbc.com/video/2021/12/21/pixar-deal-completed-to-show-disney-employees-it-was-a-new-day-says-former-ceo-bob-iger.html

Fogarty Innovation. [fogartyinnovation]. (2013, July 15). *Innovation: Thomas Fogarty and Edwards lifesciences* [Video]. *YouTube*. www.youtube.com/watch?v=J4O3sA8wDMA

Gabler, Neal. (2007). *Walt Disney: The triumph of the American imagination*. Vintage Books.

Herper, M. (2019). The astounding 19-year journey to a sea change for heart patients. *Stat News*. www.statnews.com/2019/03/19/the-astounding-19-year-journey-to-a-sea-change-for-heart-patients/

Hilal, S., & Erikson, W. (1981). Matching supplies to save lives: Linear programming the production of heart valves. *Interfaces, 11*(6), 48–56.

Iger, Robert. (2019). *The ride of a lifetime: Lessons learned from 15 years as CEO of the Walt Disney company*. Random House.

Iwerks, Leslie. (2019). *The imagineering story*. Iwerks & Co.

Matthews, A. M. (1998). The development of the Starr-Edwards heart valve. *Texas Heart Institute Journal, 25*(4), 282–293.

Mills, K. (1997, October 14). A healthier future for "the Watkins man". *Lost Angeles Times*. www.latimes.com/archives/la-xpm-1997-oct-14-fi-42633-story.html

Mussalem, Mike. (2021, August 2). *Personal interview*.

Parker, Alan. (2021). Ride of a lifetime: A conversation with Bob Iger. *Brunswick Review: The Leadership Issue*. www.brunswickgroup.com/bob-iger-disney-i19545/

Rebeiz, K. (2011). An insider perspective on implementing the Harvard Case Study Method in business teaching. *US-China Education Review A*(5), 591–601.

Rubenstein, David. (2020). The David Rubenstein show: Disney Exec. Chairman Bob Iger [Video]. *Bloomberg Presents*. www.bloomberg.com/news/videos/2020-12-03/the-david-rubenstein-show-disney-exec-chairman-bob-iger-video-ki94mqkf

Schwartzel, E., & Fritz, B. (2020). How Bob Iger unified Disney's new Magic Kingdom. *Wall Street Journal*. www.wsj.com/articles/how-bob-iger-unified-disneys-new-magic-kingdom-11582919131

Starbucks. (n.d.) *About us*. https://www.starbucksathome.com/au/story/about-us.

Volk-Weiss, Brian. (2021). *Behind the attraction*. Steve Bucks Productions; The Nacelle Company.

Watkins Incorporated. (2004). *Watkins*. Arcadia Publishing.

Index

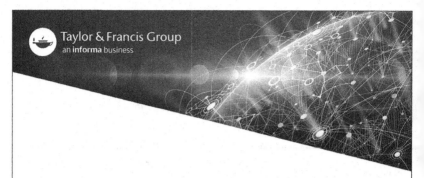

Printed in the United States
by Baker & Taylor Publisher Services